BROKER-DEALER REGULATION
IN A NUTSHELL

SECOND EDITION

By

Thomas Lee Hazen

Cary C. Boshamer Professor of Law
The University of North Carolina at Chapel Hill

A Thomson Reuters business

Mat # 40696171

Nutshell Series, In a Nutshell and the Nutshell Logo are trademarks registered in the U.S. Patent and Trademark Office.

© West, a Thomson business, 2003
© 2011 Thomson Reuters

    610 Opperman Drive
    St. Paul, MN 55123
    1–800–313–9378

Printed in the United States of America

ISBN: 978-0-314-18957-8

To
Lisa, Elliott, and George

PREFACE

The entire field of securities regulation is highly complex. Broker-dealer regulation in particular is filled with complexities and intricacies. This Nutshell is designed to provide an introduction and overview of broker-dealer regulation. The goal is to provide the reader with an understanding of basic concepts and the basic regulatory scheme. I have tried to keep citations to a minimum. The reader may want to consult additional sources for more detailed analysis of the intricacies of broker-dealer regulation (see Further Reading in the Appendix, page 257 infra). Following the Appendix at page 259, I have included a glossary of some terms that may be helpful in understanding the securities laws and broker-dealer regulations.

Significant portions of the first edition of this Nutshell were adapted from Thomas Lee Hazen, Treatise on the Law of Securities Regulation (Thomson-West 4th ed. 2002). Some material was adapted from David L. Ratner & Thomas Lee Hazen, Securities Regulation in a Nutshell (Thomson-West 7th ed. 2002). This second edition of the Nutshell contains reported developments through January 1, 2011.

Thomas Lee Hazen

Chapel Hill, North Carolina
January 2011

INTRODUCTION

This Nutshell focuses on what is generally referred to as market regulation and in particular the regulation of securities brokers and dealers. Market regulation has several layers of complex regulation. This regulation encompasses broker-dealer firms and their employees. Market regulation also extends to the stock exchanges and the over the counter markets where trading in publicly traded securities takes place.

Broker-dealer regulation addresses both "front office" and "back office" operations of broker-dealer firms (sometimes also referred to as "upstairs" and "downstairs"). The front office operations include those aspects of the brokerage firm operations that deal with the customers and the public, such as retail operations and research departments. The back office operations include the record-keeping, accounting, and clearing and settlement responsibilities of brokerage firms.

ABBREVIATIONS

1933 Act	Securities Act of 1933
1934 Act	Securities Exchange Act of 1934
AMEX	American Stock Exchange
CEA	Commodity Exchange Act
CFMA	Commodity Futures Modernization Act
CFTC	Commodity Futures Trading Commission
DMM	Designated Market Maker
FAA	Federal Arbitration Act
FinCen	Financial Crimes Enforcement Network
FINRA	Financial Industry Regulatory Authority
FRB	Federal Reserve Board
GLBA	Gramm–Leach–Bliley Act of 1999
IAA	Investment Advisers Act of 1940
ICA	Investment Company Act of 1940
IM	(NASD) Interpretive Memorandum
IPO	Initial Public Offering
ITS	Inter–Market Trading System
MSRB	Municipal Securities Rulemaking Board
NASD	National Association of Securities Dealers
NASDAQ	National Association of Securities Dealers Quotation (system)
NASDR	National Association of Securities Dealers Regulation, Inc.
NYSE	New York Stock Exchange
NYSER	New York Stock Exchange Regulation
OTC	Over-the-counter (market)

ABBREVIATIONS

PORTAL	Private Offerings, Resales and Trading through Automated Linkages
PMM	Primary Market Maker
Rel.	(SEC) Release
SAR	Suspicious Activity Report
SEC	Securities and Exchange Commission
SIPA	Securities Investor Protection Act
SIPC	Securities Investor Protection Corporation
SLUSA	Securities Litigation Uniform Standards Act
SRO	Self-regulatory organization

OUTLINE

OUTLINE

Page

TABLE OF CASES

References are to Pages

A

B

C

G

H

S

T

U

V

W

Z

TABLE OF STATUTES

UNITED STATES

UNITED STATES CODE ANNOTATED
9 U.S.C.A.—Arbitration

15 U.S.C.A.—Commerce and Trade

18 U.S.C.A.—Crimes and Criminal Procedure

31 U.S.C.A.—Money and Finance

TABLE OF STATUTES

STATUTES AT LARGE

POPULAR NAME ACTS

COMMODITY EXCHANGE ACT

FEDERAL ARBITRATION ACT

INVESTMENT ADVISERS ACT

TABLE OF STATUTES

INVESTMENT COMPANY ACT OF 1940

SECURITIES ACT OF 1933

SECURITIES EXCHANGE ACT OF 1934

SECURITIES EXCHANGE ACT OF 1934

SECURITIES EXCHANGE ACT OF 1934

SECURITIES EXCHANGE ACT OF 1934

CODE OF FEDERAL REGULATIONS

NATIONAL ASSOCIATION OF SECURITIES DEALERS CODE OF ARBITRATION

FEDERAL RULES OF CIVIL PROCEDURE

MUNICIPAL SECURITIES RULEMAKING BOARD RULES

TABLE OF STATUTES

SECURITIES AND EXCHANGE COMMISSION RULE

SECURITIES AND EXCHANGE COMMISSION RULE

SECURITIES AND EXCHANGE COMMISSION RULE

FEDERAL REGISTER

TABLE OF STATUTES

EXCHANGE ACT RELEASE

INVESTMENT ADVISORS ACT RELEASE

SECURITIES EXCHANGE ACT RELEASE

BROKER-DEALER REGULATION
IN A NUTSHELL

SECOND EDITION

CHAPTER 1

THE MARKETS AND SELF REGULATION

§ 1. Overview of the Securities Markets*

a. The Nature of Securities

Securities differ from most other commodities in which people deal. They have no intrinsic value in themselves—they represent rights in something else. The value of a bond, note or other promise to pay depends on the financial condition of the promisor. The value of a share of stock depends on the profitability or future prospects of the corporation or other entity which issued it; its market price depends on how much other people are willing to pay for it, based on their evaluation of those prospects.

The distinctive features of securities give a distinctive coloration to regulation of transactions in securities, in contrast to the regulation of transactions in other types of goods. Most goods are produced, distributed and used or consumed; governmental regulation focuses on protecting the ultimate consumer against dangerous articles, mis-

* This section is adapted from David L. Ratner & Thomas Lee Hazen, Securities Regulation in a Nutshell § 1 (7th ed. 2002).

leading advertising, and unfair or non-competitive pricing practices. Securities are different.

First, securities are created, rather than produced. They can be issued in unlimited amounts, virtually without cost, since they are nothing in themselves but represent only an interest in something else. An important focus of securities laws, therefore, is assuring that when securities are created and offered to the public, investors have an accurate idea of what that "something else" is and how much of an interest in it the particular security represents.

Second, securities are not used or consumed by their purchasers. They become a kind of currency, traded in the so-called "secondary markets" at fluctuating prices. These "secondary" transactions far outweigh, in number and volume, the offerings of newly-created securities. A second important focus of securities law, therefore, is to assure that there is a continuous flow of information about the corporation or other entity whose securities are being traded, with additional disclosure whenever security holders are being asked to vote, or make some other decision, with respect to the securities they hold.

Third, because the trading markets for securities are uniquely susceptible to manipulative and deceptive practices, all securities laws contain general "antifraud" provisions. These have been interpreted to apply not only to manipulation of securities prices, but also to trading by "insiders" on the basis of non-public information and to various kinds of misstatements by corporate management and others.

Fourth, since a large industry has grown up to buy and sell securities for investors and traders, securities laws are concerned with the regulation of people and firms engaged in that business, to assure that they do not take advantage of their superior experience and access to overreach their non-professional customers.

Finally, securities laws provide for a variety of governmental sanctions against those who violate their prohibitions, as well as civil liability to persons injured by such violations. In addition, the courts have implied the existence of civil liabilities in situations where they are not expressly provided by statute.

b. *Securities Markets*

The facilities through which securities are traded are known as "markets." These markets may have physical locations, but in many cases are simply formal or informal systems of communication through which buyers and sellers make their interests known and consummate transactions.

In terms of dollar volume, the largest securities market is the bond market—trading in the debt instruments issued by the United States government, by state and local governments, and by corporations. However, since the bond market attracts more interest from professional and institutional investors than from the general public, and since federal, state and local government obligations are exempt from most of the direct regulatory provisions of the federal securities laws, the bond markets have in recent years occupied only a small part of the attention of securities regulators.

The principal focus of securities regulation is on the markets for common stocks. There are two types of stock markets now operating in the United States—"exchange" markets and "over-the-counter" markets. An "exchange" market, of which the New York Stock Exchange (NYSE) is by far the largest, operates in a physical facility with a trading "floor" to which transactions in a particular security are directed. The orders are routed electronically through the SuperDot electronic order-routing system that links member firms to specialists' posts on the trading floor. Today, a good deal of NYSE trading takes place other than on the exchange floor, but the trading floor remains the mainstay of the exchange. For a long time, the NYSE (and, to a lesser extent, the other traditional stock exchanges) operated in a very rigid manner, prescribing the number and qualifications of members, the functions each member may perform, and (until 1975) the commission rate to be charged on all transactions. Technology changed exchange trading dramatically. Today some exchanges, such as the NASDAQ Stock market, have no physical trading floor and is a fully electronic virtual exchange. The "over-the-counter" (OTC) market, on the other hand, has traditionally been completely unstructured, without any physical facility, and with any qualified firm being free to engage in any types of activities with respect to any securities.

Until the late twentieth century, as far as the individual buyer or seller of stocks is concerned, the significant difference between an exchange and OTC transaction was the function performed by the firm with which she deals. In the case of an exchange transaction, her firm acts as a "broker"—that is, it acts as an agent for the customer's account—and charges her a commission for its services. The only person permitted to act as a "dealer" or "make a market" in the stock on the exchange floor (that is, to buy and sell the security for the dealer's own account) was the registered "specialist" in that stock. The broker transmitted the customer's order to the exchange floor where it was generally executed by buying from or selling to either the specialist or another customer whose broker has left his order on the specialist's "book."

In the OTC market, as is the case with electronic exchanges today, there is no exchange floor, only a computer and telephone communication network. The principal market for the stocks of large companies traded in the OTC market was the NASDAQ (National Association of Securities Dealers Automated Quotation) National Market System. In 2006 the NASDAQ Stock Market became a registered securities exchange but continues to operate through market-makers and electronic quotations as it did when it was an over-the-counter market. Any number of firms may act as "dealers" or "market makers" in a particular stock and may deal directly with public customers in that stock. If the firm through which a customer orders a particular stock is not a dealer in that stock, it will normally purchase it for him as a broker from one of the dealers making a market in that stock. In many cases, however, the firm will solicit orders from customers in stocks in which it is making a market, selling the stock to the customer as principal at a mark-up over the price it is currently quoting to brokers. Since retail firms commonly act simultaneously as brokers in exchange-listed stocks and as dealers in NASDAQ and OTC stocks, this may cause some confusion on the part of customers.

A firm selling stock to a customer as part of an underwritten offering of a new issue (whether of an exchange-listed or OTC stock) normally sells to the customer as principal at a fixed price (equal to or slightly below the current market price, in the case of a security which is already publicly traded). The dealer's compensation in that case comes out of the "spread" between the public offering price and the net proceeds paid to the issuer (or other person on whose behalf the distribution is being made).

c. *The Securities Industry*

The securities industry is characterized by great diversity, both in size and function. Firms registered as broker-dealers in securities range from large firms engaged in brokerage, market making, underwriting, investment advice, and fund management, as well as commodities, real estate dealings, and a variety of other financial service activities, down to one-person firms engaged solely in selling mutual fund shares or dealing in a few specialized securities.

There has always been a substantial failure rate among small securities firms, which commence operations during periods of high trading volume and fold when volume declines. In 1969 and 1970, however, as a result of operational breakdowns, unsound capital structures, and rapidly declining volume and prices for securities, there was an unprecedented series of failures of large NYSE member firms, almost causing the collapse of the industry. This near-collapse triggered a number of governmental studies, culminating in the imposition of new financial responsibility requirements on securities firms. It also led to the development of a more rational and efficient system for the clearing and settlement of securities transactions.

In 1933, as a result of the passage of the Glass–Steagall Act, which prohibited banks from dealing in securities (except government bonds), the securities industry consisted of a relatively separate and well-defined group of firms. However, with the increasing tendency for individuals to make their equity investments indirectly through institutions, rather than trading directly in stock for their own account, securities firms came increasingly into competition with banks, insurance companies, and other financial institutions. At the same time that securities firms began offering their customers an increasing number of financial services that traditionally had been associated with commercial banking, commercial banks entered into many areas that formerly were reserved for investment bankers and securities firms. This competition placed severe strains on the existing regulatory structure under which securities firms, banks, and insurance companies are regulated by different agencies with entirely different concerns and approaches. In 1999, Congress enacted the Gramm–Leach–Bliley Act (GLBA) (Pub. Law 106–102 (1999)), which repealed the Glass–Steagall Act. This paved the way for even more competition among and between financial institutions that can now offer a wide variety of financial services to its customers. The Gramm–Leach–Bliley Act adopted a system of functional regulation under which the various operations of multi-service financial institutions are regulated by different government agencies depending on the nature of the activity. Thus, for example, while securities activities of banks and other institutions are regulated by the SEC, banking activities are governed by the applicable federal or state banking agencies and insurance activities are subject to state regulation.

d.   The Securities and Exchange Commission

Securities regulation is based on a multi-layered system of self-regulation. The Securities Exchange Act of 1934 (1934 Act) established the Securities and Exchange Commission to regulate the securities markets in various respects. The 1934 Act also empowers the SEC to recognize and oversee self-regulatory organization. 1934 Act § 19.

The Securities and Exchange Commission (SEC) consists of four divisions and various offices. The division of Corporation Finance ("Corp. Fin.") has primary responsibility for examining all registration documents and reports filed with the Commission. Corp. Fin. also drafts most SEC rules and disclosure forms and guides. The Division of Trading and Markets (formerly Market Regulation) oversees the operation of the markets and broker-dealer regulation. The Division of Investment Management carries out investment company and investment adviser regulation. The Division of Enforcement conducts investigations of suspected violations and can initiate court action or administrative proceedings in appropriate cases; it also can refer matters to the Department of Justice for possible criminal prosecution. Some of the more important offices include the Office of General Counsel and the Office of the Chief Accountant.

SEC regulation is supplemented by its oversight of the self-regulatory organizations (SROs). The stock exchanges, The Financial Industry Regulatory Authority (FINRA) and formerly the National Association of Securities Dealers (NASD) are the self-regulatory organizations for the securities markets and the broker-dealers transacting business in those markets.

§ 2. How the U.S. Securities Markets Operate

The major traditional U.S. stock exchange is the NYSE. The American Stock Exchange (AMEX) trades secondary securities, as well as options.

There are also several regional exchanges that at one time only traded secondary stocks and provided regional trading for New York and American Exchange listed securities. Today some of the regional exchanges such as the Chicago, Pacific, and Philadelphia exchanges are major centers for options trading. In recent years, there have been a number of electronic facilities (electronic communications networks or ECNs) that have registered as securities exchanges under the 1934 Act. Also, in 2006 the NASDAQ Stock Market registered as an exchange.

An exchange, as the name implies, provides a central clearing house for the trading of its listed securities. Originally all transactions took place physically on the floor of the exchange. While this in some part is still true today, there has been considerable movement towards more of a national market system with automated quotations and a consolidated tape reflecting all transactions and volume whether or not the transactions are made on the exchange floor. Trading on the exchange floor traditionally was carried out by "specialists" in each listed security, whose job it was to help maintain an orderly market. By the end of the twentieth century, the mechanics of many trading processes had been automated and computerized. The specialist system has yielded to technical advances since so many trades are now done electronically. Firms that formerly operated as specialists are now known as designated market makers (DMMs). The NYSE's transition from a specialist system to one based on designated market makers means that operations on the NYSE more closely resemble trading in the NASDAQ markets than ever before.

Securities not traded on one or more of the national exchanges are traded in the over-the-counter markets that formerly were coordinated by the NASD and are now part of the NASDAQ markets. Firms that operate in the NASDAQ formerly were regulated by the NASD and now are regulated by FINRA. In the over-the-counter and NASDAQ markets, there is no central exchange floor but merely a matching of bid and asked quotes for each security. The matching of these offers to buy and offers to sell securities is carried out by market makers with respect to each security. With its national market quotation system, NASDAQ moved toward a national market system. This national market system has been successful in keeping many companies in the over-the-counter markets that in the past would have moved to the NYSE. In another attempt to strengthen its competitive position, NASDAQ acquired the AMEX. Shortly thereafter in 2003, the NASD entered into an agreement to sell AMEX to a Chicago-based private equity firm.Notwithstanding this short-lived acquisition of the American Stock Exchange, the AMEX subsequently agreed to be acquired by the NYSE. Also, the NYSE merged withArchipelago, one of the leading electronic communication networks. As a result of the NYSE–Archipelago merger, the NYSE became a publicly traded company. Subsequently the NYSE merged with Euronext—a major offshore market. NASDAQ acquired the Philadelphia Stock Exchange in 2008.

As noted above, in 2006, the NASDAQ Stock Market registered with the SEC as a securities exchange.

Prior to 1976, the exchanges prohibited transactions not taking place on the exchange (sometimes referred to as "off-board" trading) of listed securities. This prohibition has now been abolished as part of the movement towards coordinated national markets, thereby permitting off-exchange transactions in exchange-listed securities. The SEC initiated proposals for a national market system. There is not yet a single, unified national market system, and there may never be. However, strides have been made in this direction through the consolidated reports of transactions in exchange-listed securities provided by the automated Intermarket Trading System (ITS), a communications network that helps centralize activity among the exchanges. This system was supplemented by several electronic communications networks (ECNs). 1934 Act § 12 permits unlisted trading privileges through the medium of an exchange for securities listed on another exchange or traded in the over-the-counter markets. Under 1934 Act Rule 19c–3, the SEC permits off-exchange trading of exchange-listed securities.

For most of their history, the exchanges and the NASD were organized as mutual membership organizations. The NASD demutualized when it became a publicly held company. The NYSE merger with Archipeligo resulted in the NYSE's demutualization. In addition, the International Securities Exchange and the Pacific Stock Exchange have demutualized.

Following demutualization, it was necessary to separate the profit centers from the regulatory functions. As a result, the regulatory functions that formerly belonged to the NASD and the NYSE were transferred to new SROs—NASD Regulation (NASDR) and New York Stock Exchange Regulation (NYSER). In 2007, NASDR merged with NYSER to form the Financial Industry Regulatory Authority (FINRA) that carries out the functions formerly handled by NASDR and NYSER. As this book went to press, FINRA continued to work on a consolidated rulebook of regulations.

§ 3. Market Regulation—History, Background, and Overview

When Congress enacted the Securities Exchange Act of 1934, the regulation of stock brokers was not a novel concept. In fact, regulation in England dates back to the thirteenth century. By the end of the seventeenth century, legislation had been enacted to protect investors against unscrupulous manipulation by stock jobbers and stock brokers. Although the Exchange Act followed shortly on the heels of the New Deal and its response to the stock market crash of 1929, its origins predate those events. Thus, for example, there was considerable thought given to federal regulation in response to the market panic of 1907. The European experience and markets in the United States led to the 1934 Act and the current regulatory environment.

Market regulation focuses on the operation of the securities markets. This consists of regulating the trading arenas and the broker-dealer industry. Regulation thus covers the exchanges and the over-the-counter markets. There is also significant regulation covering the operation of broker-dealers and the broker-dealer industry. The concern of the securities laws in regulating exchanges and the over-the-counter markets includes organizational issues as well as trading practices. Market regulation also includes the listing standards for the various trading arenas. These listing standards include concerns about corporate governance and the way in which listed companies are operated.

The SEC does not handle the regulation of U.S. securities markets all by itself. Instead, the regulatory structure is comprised of an intricate system of self regulation. (See § 5 infra). Under this system of self regulation, the SEC oversees the exchanges (see § 6 infra) and the Financial Industry Regulatory Authority (FINRA) (see § 7 infra), which are known as self regulatory organizations (SROs).

The SEC's rulemaking power is limited with regard to market regulation. For example, the SEC's rulemaking power with respect to SROs cannot be used as a ruse for regulating substantive shareholder rights. Thus, in Business Roundtable v. SEC, 905 F.2d 406 (D.C.Cir.1990), the court invalidated the SEC's one-share-one-vote rule (1934 Act Rule 19c–4) that the SEC had claimed was supported by 1934 Act § 19(c), which sets forth SEC rulemaking and oversight responsibilities with regard to self regula-

tory organizations. The SEC thus claimed that
§ 19(c) provided an adequate statutory basis for the
rule... exists. Section 19(c) sets forth three bases
for regulation: (1) assurance of fair administration
of self-regulatory organizations, (2) conformity to
the requirements of the Exchange Act, and (3)
promulgation of rules "otherwise in furtherance of
the" Act's purpose. The SEC relied on the third
basis for its one-share-one-vote rule but the court
concluded that there was no support for a "special
and anomalous exception to the Act's otherwise
intelligible conceptual line excluding the Commission from corporate governance." (905 F.2d at 413).
The court similarly rejected the SEC's argument
that the rule could be supported by 1934 Act
§ 6(b)(5) (SEC regulatory authority over exchanges)
or by 1934 Act § 15A(b)(6) (regulatory authority
over broker-dealer associations), both of which em-
power the Commission to promulgate rules that "in
general, ... protect investors and the public interest." Additionally, 1934 Act § 11A's rulemaking
authority to "facilitate the establishment of a national market system for securities" was not a
sufficient basis for the SEC's regulation of shareholder voting rights.

There is a more detailed discussion of market
regulation in §§ 32–41 infra.

§ 4. Market Regulation and the Antitrust Laws

The federal antitrust laws are designed to curb
anticompetitive activities. Thus, for example, § 1 of

the Sherman Antitrust Act (15 U.S.C.A. § 1), among other things, prohibits contracts in restraint of trade. From time to time, the anticompetitive consequences of various activities in the securities markets have been brought into question. For example, since the definition of securities manipulation depends upon artificially pegging or fixing the price of securities, manipulative conduct by its very nature has an anticompetitive effect on securities prices. (See, e.g., Friedman v. Salomon/Smith Barney, Inc., 2000 WL 1804719, [2000–2001 Transfer Binder] Fed.Sec. L. Rep. (CCH) ¶ 91,273, 2000–2 (S.D.N.Y. 2000)). The former practice of fixed brokerage commission rates imposed by the New York Stock Exchange is another example of anticompetitive activity challenged under the antitrust laws. (See Gordon v. New York Stock Exchange, Inc., 422 U.S. 659 (1975)).

Many of the SEC and self regulatory organization rules permit conduct that otherwise would violate the antitrust laws. For example, by imposing barriers to entry, the market maker regulations limit which firms can act as market makers for over-the-counter securities. (See § 37 infra). Similarly, the specialist system for exchange-based trading was a form of permissible monopoly. (See § 35 infra).

When anticompetitive activities in the securities markets have been challenged under the antitrust laws, the response often is that the pervasive regulatory framework imposed by the securities laws on the securities markets operates as an implied repeal of the antitrust laws. The implied repeal argument has met with considerable success in challenging antitrust scrutiny of the securities markets. See, e.g., United States v. NASD, 422 U.S. 694 (1975); Gordon v. New York Stock Exchange, Inc., 422 U.S. 659 (1975).Where there is pervasive regulation either by the SEC directly or by the self regulatory organizations under the direct oversight and supervision of the SEC, the Securities Exchange Act will operate as an implied repeal of the antitrust laws. See Credit Suisse Securities (USA) LLC v. Billing, 551 U.S. 264 (2007) (public offering practices were immune from antitrust attack because of their regulation under the securities laws). On the other hand, it is clear that the antitrust laws will not be preempted simply because the alleged anticompetitive conduct involves the securities markets. Silver v. New York Stock Exchange, 373 U.S. 341 (1963).

§ 5. Self Regulation

SEC regulation of the securities industry is supplemented by a system of "self-regulation." 1934 Act §§ 6 and 15A delegate to "national securities exchanges" and "national securities associations," respectively, substantial authority over their members, including the power to expel, suspend or discipline them for certain specified kinds of activities or for "conduct ... inconsistent with just and equitable principles of trade." In order to exercise self-regulatory powers, an exchange or association must register with the SEC, which, under 1934 Act § 19, is given certain oversight powers with respect to its disciplinary proceedings and adoption and amendment of its rules.

A securities firm must become a member of one or more exchanges in order to execute transactions in listed securities on an exchange directly, and must become a member of FINRA (formerly the National Association of Securities Dealers (NASD)) to transact business effectively in the over-the-counter market. The financial crisis in the securities industry in 1969–1970 raised serious questions as to the overall effectiveness of this "self-regulatory" system, leading to SEC and Congressional reexamination of the appropriate role of industry organizations in the regulatory pattern. In addition, the distinctive features of "self-regulation" have raised a number of difficult legal questions.

a. *Disciplinary Authority*

Each self-regulatory organization has the obligation of policing its members to assure compliance with its rules and regulations. However, many of the smaller and less well-equipped exchanges found it impossible to carry out with any degree of competence their investigatory and regulatory operations. Accordingly, 1934 Act § 17(d), as amended, authorizes the SEC to allocate among the self-regulatory organizations the responsibility for being the designated examining authority for broker-dealers who are members of more than one association or exchange. The statute further allows the self-regulatory organizations by contract to agree among themselves to allocate this investigatory and inspections responsibility. Many of the smaller exchanges have availed themselves of this opportunity by contracting away their investigatory and regulatory responsibilities to the NASDR, which has since merged into FINRA. In 1996, the Act was amended to require the various examining authorities to coordinate their efforts and to eliminate "unnecessary and burdensome duplication in the examination process." (1934 Act § 17(i)).

The SROs have the authority to discipline their members, with the possible sanctions running from censure to suspension and even expulsion. Additionally, the SROs have the power to fine their members for violations. In addition to the sanctions imposed by the SROs, the SEC can institute its own disciplinary proceedings.

b. *SEC Disciplinary Authority Over Broker–Dealers*

The SEC has the power to suspend or revoke broker-dealer registration for violations of the securities laws. (1934 Act § 15(b)(5)). The SEC can also bar any person from associating with a broker-dealer (1934 Act § 15(b)(6)), a member of a registered securities association (*i.e.* FINRA) (1934 Act § 19(h)(3)), or an investment adviser (IAA § 203(f)), as well as barring that person from serving in various capacities with a registered investment company (ICA § 9(b)). In other words, the SEC can suspend or revoke an associated person's ability to work in the securities industry.

1934 Act § 15(b)(4) lists the following situations in which the SEC may impose sanctions after an administrative hearing: (1) when a broker-dealer makes false SEC filings; (2) when the broker-dealer within the past ten years has been convicted of certain crimes or misdemeanors involving moral turpitude or breaches of fiduciary duty; (3) when the person involved already has been enjoined from being a broker-dealer or investment adviser or from engaging in or continuing to engage in any conduct or practice in connection with such activity or in connection with the purchase or sale of any security; (4) when a broker-dealer has willfully violated any provision of the 1933 Act, 1934 Act, ICA, IAA, or any rules promulgated thereunder; (5) when the broker-dealer has willfully aided, abetted, counseled, commanded, induced, or procured any violation of any of these statutes or rules; (6) when the broker-dealer already is subject to an SEC order barring or suspending his right to be associated with a broker or dealer; and (7) when the broker-dealer has violated any foreign securities law or regulation.

1934 Act § 15(b)(6) empowers the Commission to impose similar sanctions for the same types of conduct with regard to persons who, although not themselves broker-dealers, are associated or seek to become associated with broker-dealers.

c. SRO Disciplinary Authority

In addition to direct SEC enforcement, the SROs have their own enforcement responsibilities. The

SROs can investigate suspected violations of self-regulatory organization rules, and accordingly discipline their members for discovered violations. SRO disciplinary authority extends to all conduct that is inconsistent with just and equitable principles of trade. Discipline is not limited to conduct that injured investors. Other types of dishonest conduct, such as misappropriation of funds from one's employer, will support disciplinary actions.

In addition to broad investigatory powers, the SROs have a wide range of disciplinary powers. SRO disciplinary actions are subject to SEC review and, in turn, to review by a federal court of appeals. Under the doctrine of exhaustion of remedies, disciplinary and other self-regulatory action must proceed through the SRO appeals process before review by the SEC or by a court. SEC approval of sanctions for violation of self-regulatory organization rules will be affirmed unless there has been an abuse of discretion.

Courts generally will not permit collateral attack as an alternative to the statutory review process for disciplinary proceedings. SROs and their employees enjoy immunity from private suits seeking damages resulting from alleged improprieties in the disciplinary process. See, e.g., Krull v. SEC, 248 F.3d 907 (9th Cir. 2001).

d.　Self–Policing

SEC regulations and self-regulation of the securities brokerage industry by SROs is supplemented by the mandate that brokerage firms police themselves. Thus, brokerage firms have a duty to supervise their personnel and can be held liable and subject to SEC or SRO sanctions for breach of the duty to supervise. (See § 27 infra).

§ 6. Stock Exchanges

When Congress created the SEC in 1934, stock exchanges, as private associations, had been regulating their members for up to one hundred and forty years. Rather than displace this system of "self-regulation," Congress superimposed the SEC on it as an additional level of regulation. 1934 Act § 5 in effect requires every "national securities exchange" to register with the SEC. 1934 Act § 6(b) provides that an exchange cannot be registered unless the SEC determines that the exchange's rules are designed, among other things, to "prevent fraudulent and manipulative acts and practices, to promote just and equitable principles of trade," and to provide for appropriate discipline of its members for any violations of its own rules or the securities laws.

Pursuant to 1934 Act § 6, the various exchanges, of which the New York Stock Exchange (NYSE) is by far the largest and most important traditional exchange, have maintained and enforced a large body of rules for the conduct of their members. As noted previously a number of electronic facilities (electronic communications networks or ECNs) have registered as securities exchanges under the 1934 Act. Also, as mentioned previously, in 2006 the NASDAQ Stock Market registered as an exchange.

Exchange rules fall into two categories: rules relating to transactions on the particular exchange, and rules relating to the internal operations of the member firms and their dealings with their customers.

The first group includes rules governing: criteria for listing securities on the exchange and provisions for delisting or suspension of trading in particular securities; obligations of issuers of listed securities; bids and offers on the exchange floor; activities of "specialists" (designated market makers in listed securities); transactions by members in listed securities for their own account; conditions under which transactions in listed securities may be effected off the exchange; clearing and settlement of exchange transactions; and rules for the governance and operation of the exchange itself.

The second category includes rules governing: the organizational structure of member firms and qualifications of their partners or officers; qualifications of salesmen and other personnel; handling of customers' accounts; advertising; and financial statements and reports. In the case of broker-dealer firms that are members of more than one exchange, there is a kind of "pecking order" with respect to regulatory responsibility.

FINRA (formerly NYSER and the NASD) has principal responsibility for regulation of the internal affairs of all of its members (which includes almost all of the largest firms in the industry). 1934 Act § 19, as originally enacted, gave the SEC power to suspend or withdraw the registration of an exchange, to suspend or expel any member of an exchange, to suspend trading in listed securities, and to require changes in exchange rules with respect to a wide range of matters. However, it did not require SEC approval for changes in stock exchange rules, nor did it provide for SEC review of disciplinary actions by exchanges against their members. 1934 Act § 19, as amended in 1975, expanded and consolidated the SEC's authority over *all* self-regulatory organizations. The SEC's authority with respect to exchanges is roughly comparable to, but even broader than, its authority over FINRA (formerly the NASD). In particular, since 1975 the SEC must give advance approval for any exchange rule changes, and it has review power over exchange disciplinary actions. The 1975 amendments also confirmed the SEC action terminating the power of exchanges to fix minimum rates of commission (which both Congress and the SEC found to have been a major cause of market distortion) and directed the SEC to eliminate any other exchange rules that imposed unwarranted restraints on competition.

§ 7. Financial Industry Regulatory Authority (FINRA) Replaces the National Association of Securities Dealers (NASD)

When Congress decided to extend federal regulation over the non-exchange, or over-the-counter (OTC) market, it followed the pattern already established with respect to exchanges. 1934 Act

§ 15A, added by the "Maloney Act" of 1938 (Pub. L. No. 75–719, 52 Stat. 1070 (1938)), authorized the establishment of "national securities associations" to be registered with the SEC. Like an exchange, any such association must have rules designed "to prevent fraudulent and manipulative acts and practices [and] to promote just and equitable principles of trade" in transactions in the OTC market. (1934 Act § 15A(b)(6)). Only one such association has been established—the NASD, which has since merged into FINRA. Prior to becoming part of FINRA, the National Association of Securities Dealer Regulation, Inc. (NASDR) was the regulatory and enforcement arm of the NASD with respect to member firms and the NASDAQ and OTC markets.

Under the authority of 1934 Act § 15A, FINRA (formerly the NASD) operates as the largest of the self-regulatory organizations subject to SEC oversight. Although the SEC has, pursuant to § 15 of the Act, the direct authority to regulate broker-dealers who are members of an SRO, as a practical matter the bulk of the day-to-day regulation is generally delegated to FINRA.

The NASD adopted a substantial body of Conduct Rules, formerly labeled "Rules of Fair Practice," dealing with various problems in the over-the-counter markets. These conduct rules are now part of FINRA'r regulations. The Conduct Rules, which are available on the FINRA website (www.finra.org), contain a general proscription that FINRA members "shall observe high standards of commercial honor and just and equitable principles of trade."

(FINRA (NASD) Conduct Rule 2110). Much fraudulent and manipulative conduct is regulated under this general proscription. FINRA also has rules directed at specific practices. Among the most important are: its rule that a dealer may not recommend a security unless it has reason to believe the security is "suitable" to the customer's financial situation and needs (FINRA (NASD) Conduct Rule 2310; see § 57 infra); its interpretation of its "fair spread or profit" rule to bar markups in excess of five percent on principal transactions (FINRA (NASD) Conduct Rule 2440, IM–2440; see § 45–46 infra); its procedures for reviewing underwriting compensation and provisions for assuring that members make a bona fide public offering of underwritten securities (FINRA Conduct Rule 5110 (formerly NASD Conduct Rule 2710)—the Corporate Finance Rule; see also FINRA Conduct Rule 5190); and its rules with respect to execution of orders in the over-the-counter market and disclosure in confirmations to customers (FINRA (NASD) Conduct Rule 2320). In addition, FINRA (formerly the NASDR) issues interpretive memoranda (IMs) explaining in more detail the standards that are expected of member firms and associated persons. IMs, rule proposals, and other announcements are announced through Notices to Members

As noted above, from time to time, FINRA promulgates rules and issues interpretations directed to specifically described prohibited practices. Although the FINRA and NASD rules and interpretations identify a number of impermissible practices, the rules and interpretations that identify specific practices are not exclusive. In other words, FINRA can invoke general antifraud principles as well as the general concept of just and equitable principles of trade to invalidate improper conduct that is not specifically defined in FINRA or SEC rulemaking.

§ 8. NASDAQ

Prior to 1971, the NASD was a purely regulatory organization, since the over-the-counter market had no central facility comparable to an exchange floor. Trading was effected by telephone calls between dealers on the basis of quotations published in commercial "sheets" by broker-dealers who chose to make markets in particular securities. However, in 1971, the NASD put into operation an electronic automated quotation system (NASDAQ) for selected over-the-counter securities, in which dealers can insert, and instantaneously update, bid and asked quotations for securities in which they are registered with FINRA and NASDAQ as market makers. NASDAQ now has both an exchange and OTC markets since the NASDAQ Stock Market became a registered securities exchange in 2006. FINRA and NASDAQ thus now combine the dual functions of an exchange: regulating access to and operation of NASDAQ, and regulating the internal affairs of those of its members that are not members of any exchange (generally the smaller firms). Under 1934 Act § 15(b)(8), as amended in 1983, a broker-dealer cannot do business in OTC securities unless it becomes a member of FINRA.

§ 9. The National Market System

The traditional structure of the securities markets, with all exchange trading taking place on the floors of the geographically dispersed national exchanges, has become outmoded. Similarly, many securities traded in the over-the-counter markets are no longer dependent on pink and yellow sheets of paper for reliable quotations in light of the emergence of NASDAQ. After extensive study, in 1975 Congress amended the 1934 Act by mandating consideration of a national market system. (See 1934 Act § 11A). The SEC's role under Section 11A includes the promulgation of rules to facilitate the consolidation of securities quotations and a national market system. Pursuant to this power, the Commission set the stage for the NASD's establishment of a national market where securities are traded similarly to what would take place on an exchange, with quotations based on the last sale rather than merely the latest bid and asked offers. Notwithstanding the similarities, the NASDAQ national market system is not based on an auction system like the national securities exchanges. Under the SEC rules, OTC securities can be listed in the NASDAQ national market in accordance with FINRA (formerly NASD) rules, provided that the issuer is sufficiently large and the shares are widely held with sufficiently high trading volume. The NASDAQ national market has been growing by leaps and bounds and now has over several thousand listed securities, including those that are now traded on the NASDAQ stock market, which is registered with the SEC as a securities exchange. Although Section 11A announced a strong directive to establish a national market system, that Section has been held not to support an implied right of action.

Although at one time eventual elimination of the exchange system appeared to have been a possible course of action, this course has not been followed. Nevertheless, the NYSE and AMEX have since each consolidated reporting of securities transactions. These systems record the price and volume for all transactions in exchange-listed stocks regardless of whether the sales take place on the exchange floor, on a regional exchange, or through NASDAQ. Additionally, 1934 Act § 12(f) permits unlisted trading privileges through the medium of an exchange for securities listed on another exchange or traded in the OTC markets. 1934 Act Rule 19c–3 permits off-exchange trading of exchange-listed securities. This does not create a single national market, but there are continuing efforts to encourage trading in securities across various markets. In addition, the SEC has had a long-standing policy that exchanges may not prevent its member broker-dealers from trading on other exchanges. (See In the Matter of the Rules of the New York Stock Exchange, 10 S.E.C. 270, 292 (1941)).

Market fragmentation remains a problem. Market fragmentation can result in gaps or inconsistences in market regulation. For example, one day in May 2010, the markets experienced a "flash crash" causing the market to tumble precipitously and then recover most of its losses within matters of hours. The SEC and the various markets instituted a study and imposed a pilot program of circuit breakers designed to prevent a reoccurrence of such extreme intra-day volatility.

§ 10. Clearing and Settlement of Securities Transactions

Clearing and settlement refers to the mechanics of executing transactions in the securities markets. Another major impact of the trend towards a central market system has been movement towards the use of a national system for clearing and settlement of securities transactions established pursuant to 1934 Act § 17A.

Congressional and SEC investigations of the securities industry's "paperwork crisis" during the period from 1968 to 1970 revealed that a substantial cause of the problem was the obsolete and inefficient method of completing transactions by the delivery (and, in some cases, cancellation and reissuance) of stock certificates. Accordingly, in the Securities Acts Amendments of 1975, Congress directed the SEC to "use its authority to facilitate the establishment of a national system for the prompt and accurate clearance and settlement of transactions in securities." (1934 Act § 17A). In furtherance of this objective, the SEC was given direct regulatory power over clearing agencies (the firms that clear securities trades) and transfer agents (who record stock transfers and the like), as well as the power to prescribe the format of securities registered under the 1934 Act. In addition to this expanded regulation, since the paperwork crisis, transfers of certificates have been reduced some-what by the establishment of a depository through which certain major brokers and banks can effect transfers among themselves without movement of certificates.

1934 Act § 17A mandates a system of uniform procedures for settlement of securities transactions by linking clearing agencies throughout the coun-try, with these clearing agencies subject to SEC registration and oversight.

§ 11. Clearing Brokers and Introducing Bro-kers

Large multi-service brokerage firms perform both retail and clearing operations themselves. However, smaller retail firms sometimes do not do their own clearing. These brokers are known as introducing brokers. Introducing brokers then contract with another firm to act as the clearing broker. As de-scribed by one court, an introducing broker "is a broker engaged in soliciting or accepting orders for the purchase or sale of any commodity for future delivery who does not accept any money, securities or property to guarantee or secure trades or con-tracts that result therefrom." (Hirshenson v. Spac-cio, 800 So.2d 670 (Fla.App.2001)). The court went on to explain, "[a]n introducing broker is generally a small broker that provides stock brokerage ser-vices and handles the substantive management of a customer's accounts. It is customary in the case of smaller brokers for another entity called the 'clearing broker' to perform mechanical, record keeping functions relating to the clearance and settlement of various transactions in the customer accounts.'' (Id.) In contrast to the role of the introducing broker, a clearing broker actually effectuates the trade. The clearing broker handles the customer funds and also operates much like a bank with respect to the transaction and the customer's funds generally.

Clearing brokers also have an obligation with respect to their clearing operations, but under most circumstances there is no further obligation. (See, e.g., Ross v. Bolton, 904 F.2d 819 (2d Cir.1990); Carlson v. Bear, Stearns & Co., 906 F.2d 315 (7th Cir.1990)). Where, however, a clearing broker has reason to know of wrongful conduct in connection with a securities transaction, the clearing broker may be held to have acted in violation of the securities laws. (See In re Bear Stearns Securities Corp., Sec. Exch. Act Rel. No. 34–41707 (SEC Aug. 5, 1999)). Thus, when there are "extenuating circumstances" and the clearing broker has knowledge of fraud by the introducing broker, the clearing broker may be held accountable. (See A.I.A. Holdings, S.A. v. Lehman Bros., Inc., 2002 WL 88226 at *3 (S.D.N.Y.2002)).

§ 12. Broker–Dealer Registration Requirements

1934 Act § 15(b)(1) requires broker-dealers to register with the SEC. 1934 Act § 15(b)(8) requires that all broker-dealers be members of a qualifying self-regulatory organization (either a national exchange or registered securities association). Additionally, most states have their own registration requirements for broker-dealers and associated persons. See §§ 19, 29 infra for further discussion of the registration requirements.

The broker-dealer registration requirements apply only to persons who, as a firm or themselves, engage in broker-dealer activities. Associated persons who work for the registered broker-dealer firm do not have to register as a broker-dealer. The exemption from the broker-dealer registration requirements does not insulate registered representatives and other associated persons from SEC regulation. Thus, for example, employees of brokerage firms who have regular contact with the public as order takers have to qualify as registered representatives with FINRA. As this Nutshell went to press, FINRA had pending proposals for registration of certain broker-dealer back office personnel. The back office personnel who would have to register include those responsible for development and approval of valuation models, employees who manage trade confirmations, account statements, trade settlement, and margin accounts, as well as employees who oversee stock loans, securities lending, prime brokerage, receipt and delivery of securities and those involved with financial or regulatory reporting.

§ 13.   Broker–Dealer Operations

In addition to regulating broker-dealer customer practices, the SEC is charged with the supervision of a firm's structure and taking measures to assure the broker-dealer's solvency. 1934 Act § 15(b)(7) requires broker-dealers to meet such operational and financial competence standards as the SEC may establish. Perhaps the most significant of these requirements is the Commission's net capital rule (1934 Act Rule 15c3–1), which sets out the minimum standards of broker-dealer solvency based on the firm's balance sheet.

a. Net Capital Rule

The net capital rule, Rule 15c3–1, is among the longest and most complex of the Commission's rules. In short, the rule requires that a broker-dealer's balance sheet reflect a sufficient asset base. The net capital rule also mandates the applicable accounting standards for determining that asset base. The net capital rule is complicated not only because of its formulas, but also because of the rules regarding "haircuts"—the discounted value of the securities before the computation is made.

b. Record–Keeping Requirements

The operational requirements imposed by the 1934 Act include provisions for maintenance of adequate records (1934 Act § 17(h)) and imposition of standards for supervisory and associated personnel. Section 17(a) of the Exchange Act requires broker-dealers to keep and furnish accurate records of their transactions. Record-keeping obligations are not limited to hard copies. They also extend to email communications. The series of SEC rules adopted under 1934 Act § 17(a) was promulgated to provide the Commission with early warning of danger signs of violations of the net capital rule or appropriate standards of broker-dealer conduct. (1934 Act Rules 17a–1 et. seq.). Violation of the record-keeping requirements does not support a private damage remedy. Touche Ross & Co. v. Redington, 442 U.S. 560 (1979). Of course, noncompliance with any of the record-keeping requirements can result in the imposition of FINRA (formerly NASD) and/or SEC sanctions. See, e.g., Everest Securities, Inc. v. SEC, 116 F.3d 1235 (8th Cir.1997). 1934 Act § 17(b) authorizes the SEC to conduct, from time to time, such "reasonable periodic, special or other examinations" as the Commission deems necessary to enforce the broker-dealer standards of operation and conduct.

c. *Customer Protection Rule*

Another important regulatory requirement is the SEC's customer protection rule, which requires segregation of customers' funds from the brokerage firm's propriety funds and accounts. (1934 Act Rule 15c3–3).

d. *Just and Equitable Principles of Trade*

The power to sanction broker-dealers for conduct that is inconsistent with just and equitable principles of trade (FINRA (formerly NASD) Conduct Rule 2110) encompasses the broker-dealers' business-related conduct generally, even if securities were not involved in the particular transactions challenged, so long as the conduct was part of their brokerage business.

§ 14. Municipal and Government Securities Dealers

None of the regulation discussed above relates to the large markets for federal, state, and local government securities. Persons who deal solely in those securities are not covered by 1934 Act § 15's regulatory structure as described above. In 1975, Congress created the Municipal Securities Rulemaking Board to regulate dealers of municipal securities. (See 1934 Act § 15B; § 30 infra). In 1986, Congress created a regulatory structure for dealers in federal government securities such as Treasury bonds, bills and notes. (See 1934 Act § 15C; § 31 infra).

§ 15. Banking and the Securities Laws

At the end of the twentieth century, a major change in securities regulation was the integration of various financial services. Until 1999, the Glass–Steagall Act prohibited national banks from dealing in investment securities. The GLBA repealed the Glass–Steagall barriers between commercial and investment banking. Even prior to its repeal, Glass–Steagall's separation of commercial and investment banking eroded. For example, bank holding companies acquired discount brokerage services. Several full service brokerage firms purchased regional banks. There is ever-increasing competition between banks and broker-dealers with money market funds and interest-bearing checking accounts. A

related development was the acquisition of brokerage firms by companies offering other financial services, such as banks and insurance companies.

§ 16.   Anti–Money Laundering Provisions

As major financial institutions, broker-dealers are
frequently used by the unscrupulous to engage in
money laundering operations. The activities that
can lead to money laundering generally include
organized crime operations, drug trafficking, and
financial fraud. There are several federal statutes
that address illegal money laundering operations.
E.g., 18 U.S.C.A. § 1952 (the Travel Act); 31
U.S.C.A. §§ 5311–5213 (Foreign Corrupt Practices
Act); 31 U.S.C.A. § 5313(a); 31 C.F.R. § 103.22(a)
(Bank Secrecy Act). As a result of increased efforts
to enforce the federal anti-money laundering rules,
broker-dealers, like other financial institutions, are
subject to regulations and compliance programs designed to detect and, in turn, prevent money laundering operations from being filtered through these
institutions. The required compliance programs include reporting of certain transactions. 31 U.S.C.A.
§ 5318(g).

In 2002, the NYSE and the NASD set forth rules
designed to strengthen their anti-money laundering
compliance programs. Sec. Exch. Act Rel. No. 34–
45487, 2002 WL 347704 (SEC Feb. 28, 2002). In
particular, these rules require member firms to
establish compliance programs that at a minimum:
(1) establish and implement policies and procedures
that can be reasonably expected to detect and cause

the reporting of transactions required under 31 U.S.C.A. § 5318(g); (2) establish and implement policies, procedures, and internal controls reasonably designed to achieve compliance with the Bank Secrecy Act; (3) provide for independent testing for compliance to be conducted by members or member organization personnel or by a qualified outside party; (4) designate and identify to the Exchange (by name, title, mailing address, e-mail address, telephone number, and facsimile number) a person or persons responsible for implementing and monitoring the day-to-day operations and internal controls of the program and provide prompt notification to the Exchange regarding any change in such designation(s); and (5) provide ongoing training for appropriate persons. FINRA and the exchanges now require broker-dealers to establish anti-money laundering compliance programs.

In the wake of the terror attacks of September 11, 2001, Congress enacted the USA Patriot Act (Pub. L. No. 107–56 (2001)), which, among other things, broadens the list of financial institutions subject to the anti-money laundering laws. The Treasury Department promulgated rules implementing the new provisions. 31 C.F.R. Part 103.

On July 1, 2002, The Financial Crimes Enforcement Network (FinCEN) announced some new reporting rules. The rules require brokers to report suspicious transactions that are conducted or attempted by, at, or through a broker-dealer and involve or aggregate at least $5,000 in funds or other assets. Specifically, the rules identify four classes of transactions that qualify as involving suspicious activity. First, suspicious activity includes transactions involving funds derived from illegal activity or intended or conducted in order to hide or disguise funds derived from illegal activity. Second, the rule covers transactions designed, whether through structuring or other means, to evade the requirements of the Bank Secrecy Act. The third category consists of transactions that appear to serve no business or apparent lawful purpose or are not the sort of transactions in which the particular customer would be expected to engage, and for which the broker-dealer knows of no reasonable explanation after examining the available facts. The fourth type of transaction that qualifies as suspicious activity includes transactions intended to further a criminal purpose, but apparently involving legally-derived funds. This fourth category is directed to cover the use of the broker-dealer to facilitate criminal activity, including terrorism.

The reporting requirements apply to broker-dealers dealing in security futures products, but the rules do not apply to futures commission merchants subject exclusive jurisdiction of the Commodity Futres Trading Commission (CFTC). Firms required to register as broker-dealers solely to permit the sale of variable annuities of life insurance companies are required to report suspicious transactions. Also, the rules apply to broker-dealers, even if they are affiliates or subsidiaries of banks or bank holding companies. In order to ensure that bank-affiliated broker-dealers are not also subject to the SAR requirement applicable to subsidiaries of bank holding companies, FinCEN requested that the federal banking supervisory agencies amend their regulations to exempt broker-dealers from having to report suspicious transactions in Suspicious Activity Reports (SARs) under rules adopted pursuant to Title 12 of the U.S. Code.

The rules adopted by FinCen include an exception from the reporting requirement for reporting for robbery or burglary. The rules further avoid double reporting by providing that only one report need be filed for a particular transaction. The rule provides that the obligation to identify and report a suspicious transaction rests with each broker-dealer involved in the transaction, but that only one SAR–BD filing is required. The responsibility of overseeing compliance with the SAR reporting requirements rests with the SEC or other applicable regulatory agency.

The FinCen rules require broker-dealers to employ a risk-based approach to monitoring activity for suspicious transactions and that the "reason-to-suspect" standard means that "on the facts existing at the time, a reasonable broker-dealer in similar circumstances would have suspected the transaction was subject to SAR reporting."

§ 17. Overview of Market Manipulation

In the hearings which led to enactment of the 1934 Exchange Act, one of the most serious abuses in the securities markets on which Senate investigators focused was the operation of "pools" which ran up the prices of securities on an exchange by a series of well-timed transactions, effected solely for the purpose of "manipulating" the market price of the security, then unloaded their holdings on the public just before the price dropped. Accordingly, 1934 Act §§ 9 and 10(a) prohibit a variety of manipulative activities with respect to exchange-listed securities, and § 10(b) contains a catch-all provision permitting the SEC to prohibit by rule any "manipulative or deceptive device or contrivance" with respect to any security.

a.   *1934 Act § 10*

1934 Act § 10(a) prohibits "short sales" and "stop loss" orders in violation of SEC rules. 1934 Act § 10(b), which is much broader, provides that it is unlawful "to use or employ [utilizing any means or instrumentality of interstate commerce], in connection with the purchase or sale of any security * * * any manipulative or deceptive device or contrivance in contravention of such rules and regulations as the Commission may prescribe as necessary or appropriate in the public interest or for the protection of investors." The SEC, following the legislative mandate, has invoked its rulemaking authority to prohibit a wide variety of conduct; the most notable is 1934 Act Rule 10b–5 (see § 18 infra).

b.   *The Section 10(b) Rules*

1934 Act Rule 10b–1 applies the prohibitions against market manipulation contained in 1934 Act

§ 9(a) to securities that are exempt from 1934 Act § 12's registration requirements.

1934 Act Rule 10b–3 prohibits broker-dealers from engaging in manipulative or deceptive acts and practices with regard to securities not traded on a national exchange and with regard to municipal securities. Rule 10b–3 thus closes a large part of the gap left by 1934 Act § 9, which applies its anti-manipulation provisions only to transactions effected through a national exchange.

1934 Act Rule 10b–5 is the broadest of the Section 10(b) rules, as it prohibits material misstatements and omissions as well as fraudulent acts in connection with purchases and sales of securities; it supports a broad implied private right of action. Rule 10b–5 is considered in the following section.

Former 1934 Act Rule 10b–6, which is now part of SEC Regulation M (see § 52 infra), prohibited purchases during a distribution of securities by persons participating in the distribution unless those persons were engaged in certain stabilizing activities. Former Rules 10b–7 and 10b–8 were also incorporated into Regulation M.

1934 Act Rule 10b–9 prohibits "all or none" offerings of securities unless all such securities are "sold at a specified price within a specified time, and * * * the total amount due to the seller is received by him by a specified date." The rule imposes the same requirements for offerings where all or part of the purchase price will be refunded if the offering is not fully subscribed.

1934 Act Rule 10b–10 requires that brokers confirm all transactions in writing. Among other things, the confirmation must disclose the broker's commission and whether he or she is acting as principal or as an agent for someone other than the customer.

1934 Act Rule 10b–16 requires disclosure of credit terms in connection with margin transactions. (See § 26 infra).

1934 Act Rule 10b–17 prohibits untimely announcements of dividends, stock splits, reverse stock splits, and rights or subscription offerings. The announcement must comply with applicable exchange rules or must be given to FINRA (formerly the NASD) at least ten days prior to the record date and must describe the nature of the distribution or offering.

1934 Act Rule 10b–18 sets out a safe harbor rule that permits a company to purchase of its own shares its own shares in market transactions.

§ 18. Overview of the Antifraud Provisions*

A vast amount of broker-dealer regulation is based on the securities laws' general antifraud provisions. What follows is a summary of the most important provisions.

* Portions of this section are adapted from David L. Ratner & Thomas Lee Hazen, Securities Regulation in a Nutshell § 17 (7th ed. 2002) and 4 Thomas Lee Hazen, Treatise on the Law of Securities Regulation ch. 12 (6th ed. 2009). See id. for further discussion of the antifraud provisions.

a.   1934 Act § 10(b) and 1934 Act Rule 10b–5

1934 Act § 10(b) is a catch-all provision, designed to deal with abuses that escaped the specific prohibitions of 1934 Act §§ 9 and 10(a). It makes it unlawful for any person to use the mails or facilities of interstate commerce:

"To use or employ, in connection with the purchase or sale of any security * * * any manipulative or deceptive device or contrivance in contravention of such rules and regulations as the Commission may prescribe as necessary or appropriate in the public interest or for the protection of investors."

1934 Act § 10(b) is not self-executing since by its terms it does not make anything unlawful unless the Commission has adopted a rule prohibiting it.

In 1942, the Commission was presented with a situation in which the president of a company was buying shares from the existing shareholders at a low price by misrepresenting the company's financial condition. While 1933 Act § 17(a) prohibits fraud and misstatements in the sale of securities, the 1933 Act does not contain a comparable provision prohibiting such practices in connection with the purchase of securities. The SEC's Assistant Solicitor accordingly lifted the operative language out of § 17(a), made the necessary modifications, added the words "in connection with the purchase or sale of any security," and presented the product to the Commission as 1934 Act Rule 10b–5. It was unanimously approved without discussion. Remarks of Milton Freeman, 22 Bus. Lawyer 922 (1967).

As adopted (and it has not been amended), Rule 10b–5 states:

"It shall be unlawful for any person, directly or indirectly, by the use of any means or instrumentality of interstate commerce, or of the mails, or of any facility of any national securities exchange,

"(a) to employ any device, scheme, or artifice to defraud,

"(b) to make any untrue statement of a material fact or to omit to state a material fact necessary in order to make the statements made, in the light of circumstances under which they were made, not misleading, or

"(c) to engage in any act, practice, or course of business which operates or would operate as a fraud or deceit upon any person,

"in connection with the purchase or sale of any security."

In the 56 years since its adoption, this simple rule has been invoked in countless SEC and private proceedings, and applied to almost every conceivable kind of situation.

In the 1960s and early 1970s, many federal appellate courts and district courts developed expansive interpretations of Rule 10b–5 (and other antifraud provisions of the securities laws). They applied it to impose liability for negligent as well as deliberate misrepresentations, for breaches of fiduciary duty by corporate management, and for failure by directors, underwriters, accountants, and lawyers to prevent wrongdoing by others. In private actions for damages, the courts were willing to imply a private right of action in anyone whose losses were even remotely connected with the alleged wrongdoing, or even in someone who had suffered no loss if her suit would help to encourage compliance with the law. The Supreme Court aided and abetted this development, giving an expansive reading to the terms "fraud" and "purchase or sale" and to the "connection" that had to be found between them.

Starting in 1975, a new conservative majority on the Supreme Court sharply reversed this trend in a series of decisions giving a narrow reading to the terms of Rule 10b–5 and other antifraud provisions, and limiting the situations in which a private right of action will be implied. The tone of these recent Supreme Court decisions is even more important than their actual holdings. They cast doubt on the continued vitality of many of the expansive decisions prior to 1975, even those that have not been specifically overruled. This fact should be kept in mind in evaluating the discussion in the following sections, which summarize the current law governing the application of the rule.

(1) Elements of a Rule 10b–5 Violation

There are three separate clauses in Rule 10b–5, not arranged in a very logical order. Clauses (a) and (c) speak in terms of "fraud" or "deceit" while clause (b) speaks in terms of misstatements or omissions. It is generally assumed, however, that clause (c), which prohibits "any act, practice, or course of business which operates or would operate as [1] a fraud or deceit [2] upon any person [3] in connection with [4] the purchase or sale [5] of any security," has the broadest scope. Each of the five elements of this formulation has given rise to interpretive questions.

"Fraud or Deceit." **Rule 10b–5 is** an "antifraud" provision. It was adopted by the SEC under authority of a section designed to prohibit "any manipulative or deceptive device or contrivance," and two of its three operative clauses are based on the concept of "fraud" or "deceit." The Supreme Court has held that no person can be found to have violated Rule 10b–5, in either an SEC or a private action, unless he is shown to have acted with "scienter." Aaron v. SEC, 446 U.S. 680 (1980); Ernst and Ernst v. Hochfelder, 425 U.S. 185 (1976). The scienter requirement, in the view of some courts, does not require that the person acted willfully, but may be met by showing that he acted recklessly. See, e.g., Tellabs, Inc. v. Makor Issues & Rights, Ltd., 551 U.S. 308 (2007); Employers Teamsters Local Nos. 175 and 505 Pension Trust Fund v. Clorox Co., 353 F.3d 1125, 1134 (9th Cir. 2004); Sanders v. John Nuveen, 554 F.2d 790 (7th Cir. 1977). Interestingly, the Supreme Court has held that a violation of clause (2) or (3) of 1933 Act § 17(a) (from which the language of the corresponding clauses of Rule 10b–5 was adapted) can be established without showing scienter. Aaron v. SEC,

supra. Thus, the language of clauses (b) and (c) of Rule 10b–5, because it is based on 1934 Act § 10(b), has a different meaning than the corresponding language in 1933 Act § 17(a).

A recurrent problem in litigation under Rule 10b–5 has been whether the complaint meets the requirements of Rule 9(b) of the Federal Rules of Civil Procedure, which states that, in cases alleging fraud, the circumstances constituting fraud must be "stated with particularity." See, e.g., O'Brien v. National Property Analysts Partners, 936 F.2d 674 (2d Cir. 1991). In the Private Securities Litigation Reform Act of 1995, Congress provided that, where liability requires "proof that the defendant acted with a particular state of mind, the complaint shall * * * state with particularity facts giving rise to a strong inference that the defendant acted with the required state of mind." 1934 Act § 21D(b). The Act also provides that, where liability of any defendant for money damages depends on his state of mind, the court, on defendant's request, must "submit to the jury a written interrogatory on the issue of each such defendant's state of mind at the time the alleged violation occurred." 1934 Act § 21D(d).

"Upon Any Person." Since the SEC's rule-making power under 1934 Act § 10(b) is to be exercised "for the protection of investors," it can be argued that the only persons entitled to the protection of Rule 10b–5 are those who can be classified as "investors." However, the definition has been stretched in a number of ways. One of the most important came in Hooper v. Mountain States, 282

involving a misappropriation of the proceeds (see In re Investors Funding, 523 F.Supp. 563 (S.D.N.Y. 1980)), and that there is no liability when there is a substantial time gap or no direct causal link between the sale and the alleged fraud. See Ketchum v. Green, 557 F.2d 1022 (3d Cir. 1977); Rochelle v. Marine Midland, 535 F.2d 523 (9th Cir. 1976).

An important decision for broker-dealers is SEC v. Zandford, 535 U.S. 813 (2002), wherein the SEC sued a stock broker who emptied his client's account and converted the proceeds. The defendant contended that since there was no fraud in connection with specific securities transactions, Rule 10b–5 could not be used to challenge the broker's actions; the Second Circuit agreed with the defendant's argument. The Supreme Court rejected this analysis, reasoning that the purpose of the federal securities laws was to assure the existence of honest securities markets and to promote investor confidence. The Court explained that there was deception and that 1934 Act § 10(b) applied. The Court reasoned that since the broker failed to disclose the challenged embezzlement from a securities account, this material omission was a sufficient connection to establish securities fraud. The *Zandford* decision is significant in that it establishes a broad test for the reach of the securities laws. Rather than simply focus on a specific transaction, if the fraud involves securities in any meaningful way, then the securities laws are implicated. It is also noteworthy that the Justices who are generally divided in securities decisions were unanimous in the *Zandford* holding.

Another important extension of the "in connection with" language came in SEC v. Texas Gulf Sulphur, 401 F.2d 833 (2d Cir. 1968) which gave an expansive interpretation of the types of statements that could trigger Rule 10b–5 liability. In that case, the court held that misstatements in a press release issued by a publicly-held corporation, which was not at the time engaged in buying or selling any of its own shares, violated Rule 10b–5 because they were made "in connection with" the purchases and sales being made by shareholders in the open market. This holding has formed the basis for a large number of shareholder class actions, alleging damages suffered because of misstatements in a company's reports or press releases. The Second Circuit has continued to give an expansive reading. For example, the court held that an advertisement for a drug that appeared in a medical journal could be found to have been made "in connection with the purchase or sale" of a security. In re Carter–Wallace, Inc. Securities Litigation, 150 F.3d 153 (2d Cir. 1998).

"Purchase or Sale." In the *Hooper* case, supra, the court held that the issuance by a corporation of its own shares was a "sale" under Rule 10b–5. In its first decision interpreting Rule 10b–5, the Supreme Court held that a merger involved a "sale" of the stock of the disappearing company and a "purchase" of the stock of the surviving company for the purposes of the rule. SEC v. National Securities, 393 U.S. 453 (1969). Other types of reorganizations may or may not be considered a "sale." Compare International Controls v. Vesco, 490 F.2d 1334 (2d

Cir. 1974), holding a spin-off of a subsidiary to be a sale, with In re Penn Central, 494 F.2d 528 (3d Cir. 1974), holding an exchange of shares of an operating company for those of a newly-formed holding company not to be a sale.

An oral option to purchase a security satisfies Rule 10b–5's purchase or sale requirement. Wharf Limited v. United International, 532 U.S. 588 (2001). This is true even when the alleged fraud is a secret intention not to honor the rights of the option holder. Id.

The Supreme Court has held that a pledge of securities is a "sale" for purposes of the 1933 Act, since 1933 Act § 2(a)(3) defines "sale" to include "every contract of sale or disposition of a security or interest in a security, for value." Rubin v. United States, 449 U.S. 424 (1981). It is unclear whether a similar result would be reached under the 1934 Act, since 1934 Act § 3(a)(14) defines "sale" only to include "any contract to sell or otherwise dispose of." See Mallis v. FDIC, 568 F.2d 824 (2d Cir. 1977), cert. dismissed, 435 U.S. 381 (1978).

"Of Any Security." Rule 10b–5 applies to any purchase or sale by any person of any security. There are no exemptions. It applies to securities which are registered under the 1934 Act, or which are not so registered. It applies to publicly-held companies, to closely-held companies, and to any kind of entity which issues something that can be called a "security." Security is broadly defined to include a wide range of investment opportunities beyond stocks and bonds. *See, e.g.,* SEC v. W.J.

Howey Co., 328 U.S. 293 (1946). Rule 10b–5 even applies to "exempted securities," as defined in 1934 Act § 3(a)(12) (including federal, state and local government securities), which are specifically exempted from certain other provisions of the Act. The Supreme Court's rejection of the "sale of business" doctrine, see § 6(b) supra, means that this will probably continue to be the case, despite occasional complaints from judges that Congress could not have intended these local and private disputes to be decided in the federal courts. See Trecker v. Scag, 679 F.2d 703 (7th Cir. 1982) (Posner, J., concurring).

Materiality. Materiality is a key concept under the securities laws generally and also is the benchmark for determining when a misstatement or omission can violate Rule 10b–5. In TSC v. Northway, 426 U.S. 438 (1976), the Supreme Court explained that "an omitted fact is material if there is a substantial likelihoodthat a reasonable shareholder would consider it important in deciding how to vote * * *." Put another way, there must be a substantial likelihood that the disclosure of the omitted fact would have been viewed by the reasonable investor as having significantly altered the 'total mix' of information made available. This standard is not limited to omissions and thus applies as well to determining the materiality of a misstatement.

(2) *Civil Liability for Rule 10b–5 Violations*

Rule 10b–5 is worded as a prohibition; there is no express provision anywhere in the securities laws prescribing any civil liability for its violation. However, starting in 1946, courts have been applying to it the common law tort rule that a person who violates a legislative enactment is liable in damages if he invades an interest of another person that the legislation was intended to protect. Kardon v. National Gypsum, 69 F.Supp. 512 (E.D.Pa. 1946). This question of the existence of an "implied private right of action" for violations of the rule did not reach the Supreme Court until 1971, at which time the Court simply stated in a footnote, without discussion, that "a private right of action is implied under § 10(b)." While the Court, in more recent decisions, has questioned the rationale for implying private rights of actions under the federal securities laws (see § 36 infra), it has not thus far indicated any intention to reexamine the availability of such a right under Rule 10b–5. In fact, the Court has reaffirmed Rule 10b–5's implied remedy.

Overlap with Other Provisions. Recognition of a private right of action for fraudulent misstatements under Rule 10b–5 raises the possibility that any such action may be brought where the misstatement is covered by another, more specific, provision of federal securities law. In SEC v. National Securities, 393 U.S. 453 (1969), the Supreme Court held that Rule 10b–5 could be applied to misstatements in proxy statements, even though proxy solicitation was governed by specific SEC rules under 1934 Act § 14. Subsequently, the Court has held that suit can be brought under Rule 10b–5 to recover damages resulting from misstatements in a 1933 Act registration statement, even though such misstatements give rise to a specific right of action under 1933 Act § 11. Herman & MacLean v. Huddleston, 459 U.S. 375 (1983). Lower courts have also held that such suits can be brought with respect to misstatements in documents filed under the 1934 Act, even though there could also be specific civil liability under 1934 Act § 18 for material misstatements and omissions in SEC filings. See Ross v. A.H. Robins, 607 F.2d 545 (2d Cir. 1979).

The "Purchaser–Seller" Requirement. The most significant court-imposed limitation on private litigation under Rule 10b–5 is the requirement that the plaintiff be either a "purchaser" or "seller" of securities in the transaction being attacked. In Birnbaum v. Newport, 193 F.2d 461 (2d Cir. 1952), one of the earliest cases under Rule 10b–5, the court held that the purpose of the rule was to protect purchasers and sellers of securities from being defrauded, and that since neither the minority shareholders nor the corporation had purchased or sold any securities, they had no cause of action.

The "purchaser-seller" requirement of *Birnbaum* was reaffirmed by the Supreme Court in Blue Chip v. Manor, 421 U.S. 723 (1975). In *Blue Chip*, defendants were obliged under an antitrust decree to offer plaintiffs certain shares in a new company. Plaintiffs alleged that defendants had violated Rule 10b–5 by giving a deceptively pessimistic portrayal of the new company in the prospectus, for the purpose of inducing the plaintiffs not to buy the shares. While the facts were highly unusual, the court rested its decision to deny standing to any person other than a purchaser or seller on the broad policy ground that it would deter "vexatious litigation" which "may have a settlement value out of any proportion to its prospect of success at trial" and which may raise "many rather hazy issues of historical fact the proof of which depend[s] almost entirely on oral testimony." Justice Rehnquist's majority opinion is replete with expressions of hostility towards private actions against corporate management. This hostility to private rights of action led dissenting Justice Blackmun to remark that "the Court exhibits a preternatural solicitousness for corporate well-being and a seeming callousness toward the investing public quite out of keeping * * * with our own tradition and the intent of the securities laws."

One important exception to the purchaser-seller requirement is that a person whose shares are automatically converted into shares of another company in a merger put through by means of misleading statements is entitled to sue under Rule 10b–5 as a "forced seller." Vine v. Beneficial Finance, 374 F.2d 627 (2d Cir. 1967). Courts have continued to apply the "forced seller" exception after the Supreme Court decision in *Blue Chip*. See Alley v. Miramon, 614 F.2d 1372, 1387 (5th Cir. 1980). However, the forced seller doctrine is narrowly interpreted. See Jacobson v. AEG Capital Corp., 50 F.3d 1493, 1499 (9th Cir. 1995) ("forced sale doctrine does not cut a wide swath").

Causation. In actions under Rule 10b–5, courts have generally held that the plaintiff must show both "transaction causation," i.e., that the fraud caused the plaintiff to enter into the transaction, and "loss causation," i.e., that the transaction caused the loss to the plaintiff. See, e.g., Schlick v. Penn–Dixie, 507 F.2d 374 (2d Cir. 1974). More recently, some courts have gone further and required that the plaintiff demonstrate that the loss was a result of the facts which were misrepresented by the defendant. See, e.g., Bastian v. Petren, 892 F.2d 680 (7th Cir. 1990). Congress in 1995 codified this approach by providing that in any private action under the 1934 Act, "the plaintiff shall have the burden of proving that the act or omission of the defendant alleged to violate the Act caused the loss for which the plaintiff seeks to recover damages." 1934 Act § 21D(b)(4).

Reliance. Reliance ordinarily is an element of any fraud claim. When dealing with claims against broker-dealers, customers generally will have to establish actual reliance and also that the reliance was reasonable. With respect to securities class actions, an important question is whether a plaintiff must show that he or she actually relied on the misleading statement when the plaintiff purchased or sold the securities at issue. In 1975, the Ninth Circuit held that the issuance of a misleading statement constitutes a "fraud on the market." Under this approach, the plaintiff need not show that he or she actually relied on the misleading statement; the plaintiff need only show that he or she bought or sold at a price which was affected by the statement. Blackie v. Barrack, 524 F.2d 891 (9th Cir.1975). In 1988, the Supreme Court, in a 4–2 decision with 3 justices not participating, upheld the application of the "fraud on the market" theory to establish a rebuttable presumption of reliance. Basic v. Levinson, 485 U.S. 224 (1988).

Damages. Since the corporation which is being sued in these cases has generally not engaged in transactions with the plaintiff, courts have held that an "out of pocket" measure of damages is appropriate. See, e.g., Huddleston v. Herman, 640 F.2d 534 (5th Cir. 1981); Green v. Occidental, 541 F.2d 1335 (9th Cir. 1976) (Sneed, J., concurring). Alternatives to out of pocket damages could include benefit of the bargain which will not ordinarily be available under Rule 10b–5.

b.   *1934 Act § 15(c)(1)*

1934 Act § 15(c)(1) gives the SEC power to promulgate rules prohibiting brokers and dealers from engaging in "manipulative, deceptive, or otherwise fraudulent" devices and contrivances.

c.   *The § 15(c) Rules*

1934 Act Rule 15c1–2 prohibits fraud and misrepresentation by including conduct that operates as a fraud and material misstatements and omissions within section 15(c)'s purview.

1934 Act Rule 15c1–3 prohibits brokers and dealers from implying that the SEC has reviewed their financial standing and/or business practices.

Under 1934 Act Rule 15c1–5, broker-dealers, including municipal securities dealers, who control or are controlled by the issuer of a security cannot enter a customer's transaction without disclosing the control relationship.

1934 Act Rule 15c1–6 requires brokers and dealers participating or interested in a distribution to fully disclose such participation or interest.

1934 Act Rule 15c1–7 prohibits excessive trading in order to charge of excessive fees in connection with discretionary accounts and requires prompt disclosure of all transactions made on behalf of discretionary accounts. Excessive trading to generate commissions is also known as "churning." (See § 68 infra).

1934 Act Rule 15c1–8 prohibits sales "at the market" unless the broker or dealer has a reasonable belief that a market exists.

1934 Act Rule 15c1–9 prohibits brokers and dealers from disseminating pro forma financial statements with regard to issuers and their securities unless the assumptions underlying the pro forma figures are explicitly disclosed and explained.

1934 Act Rule 15c2–1 prohibits brokers and dealers from hypothecating customers' securities and certain commingling of securities held by the broker-dealer for the customer.

1934 Act Rule 15c2–4 requires prompt transmission by brokers and dealers of all funds or other consideration received in connection with underwriting activities.

1934 Act Rule 15c2–5 requires disclosures of the terms and risks associated with securities transactions on credit. Extension of credit is regulated by Federal Reserve Board Regulation T. Compliance with Regulation T's margin procedures will satisfy Rule 15c2–5.

In 1990, the SEC adopted 1934 Act Rule 15c2–6, which was known as the penny stock rule and covered broker-dealer recommendations of many over-the-counter securities trading at less than five dollars, provided that the security was not listed on an exchange or traded through NASDAQ. The rule imposed disclosure, know-your-customer, and suitability obligations with regard to transactions in such low priced stocks entered into on the basis of the broker-dealer's recommendation. In 1992, the Commission adopted more comprehensive penny stock regulation in 1934 Act Rules 15g–1 through 15g–6; these rules replaced the former Rule 15c2–6.

1934 Act Rule 15c2–7 generally requires all market quotations to be properly identified, including the identity of the broker or dealer placing the quotation. The rule thus prohibits "fictitious" quotations. Also, the rule requires, for example, disclosure to the applicable inter-dealer quotation system that any quotation is properly being entered on behalf of another broker-dealer or is entered pursuant to an arrangement with other broker-dealers.

1934 Act Rule 15c2–8 establishes what constitutes proper conduct relating to brokers' and dealers' prospectus delivery obligations under the Securities Act of 1933. Rule 15c2–11 prohibits brokers or dealers from entering or resuming quotations in securities unless adequate current public information is available concerning the security and issuer. There is a safe harbor for determining whether the public information is reasonably current.

The foregoing prohibitions and disclosure requirements supplement the rules of FINRA (formerly the NASD) and the stock exchanges as well as those of the Municipal Securities Rulemaking Board (MSRB).

§ 19.   State Regulation; Limited Preemption

There is a considerable body of state law that supplements federal regulation by the SEC and the SROs. State securities laws, often referred to as "Blue Sky Laws," impose extensive regulatory and customer protection rules on the securities industry. State law respecting fiduciary duties may also be applied to broker-dealers under appropriate circumstances. In addition, state contract law will govern many aspects of the customer-broker relationship.

In 1996, Congress, as part of the National Securities Markets Improvement Act of 1996 (Pub. L. No. 104–290, 110 Stat. 3416 (1996)), took away from the states the power to regulate certain areas of broker-dealer activity. In particular, the states may not impose regulations relating to the extension of credit (margin requirements) (see § 26 infra), net capital requirements (see § 25 infra), or recordkeeping and reporting requirements (see § 13 supra). In addition to this limited preemption of substantive state regulation, class actions based on securities fraud are preempted by the Securities Litigation Uniform Standards Act of 1998 (Pub. Law No. 105–353, 112 Stat. 3227 (1998)).

Notwithstanding this preemptive legislation, many states play a significant role in broker-dealer regulation. For example, a number of states and local district attorneys have been aggressive in enforcing state antifraud provisions in broker-dealer prosecutions. States have also been active in pursuing conflicts of interest that exist within the broker-dealer industry—most notably the conflicts involving research analysts (see § 61 infra).

CHAPTER 2

BROKER–DEALER DEFINITIONS AND REGISTRATION REQUIREMENTS

§ 20. Broker–Dealer Registration Requirements

1934 Act § 15(a)(1) requires securities brokers and dealers to be registered in order to conduct their business, unless their business is exclusively intrastate or unless otherwise exempted from registration.

a. Registration Generally

Subject to certain exemptions, the 1934 Act requires registration with the SEC of broker-dealer firms that conduct business in interstate commerce. Registration subjects the firm to many reporting requirements also impacts their daily operation and organizational structure.

The broker-dealer registration requirements are found in 1934 Act § 15(b) and the SEC rules promulgated thereunder. The registration process is commenced by an applicant's completion of SEC Form BD. The information to be supplied in the registration materials includes a detailed description of the broker-dealer's assets and financial condition, including a showing of compliance with the Commission's net capital rule which imposes minimum solvency requirements on broker-dealer firms. Nonresident broker-dealers, general partners of broker-dealers, and managing agents of broker-dealers must file an irrevocable power of attorney designating the SEC as agent for service of process.

After the Form BD has been filed, the SEC may grant or deny the registration. In the event that the SEC is inclined to deny an application for registration, it is directed by statute to institute formal proceedings by giving notice of the grounds for the proposed denial and giving the applicant an opportunity to be heard. Once a broker-dealer's registration has been granted, the SEC can also institute formal proceedings to revoke the registration for noncompliance with the registration or other requirements of the Act. The SEC may suspend a broker-dealer's registration pending a determination of whether the registration should be revoked. As an alternative to ordering a revocation of registration, the SEC has the option of censuring or placing limitations upon the broker-dealer's activities for less severe violations such as minor recordkeeping infractions. Additionally, the SEC may suspend a broker-dealer for a period of up to one year.

Once a broker-dealer is registered under the Act, cancellation may be effected by filing a formal withdrawal from registration. Registration can also be suspended or revoked as a result of disciplinary action by the SEC or an SRO such as FINRA.

In addition to setting forth § 15's registration requirements, the 1934 Act makes it unlawful for a broker-dealer to engage in business involving interstate commerce unless the broker-dealer is a member of a national exchange or FINRA (formerly the NASD). Holding oneself as registered under the Act is fraudulent in the absence of a bona fide registered status. In addition to the SEC's registration requirements, FINRA and other SROs, the exchanges, and state governments may impose their own registration requirements.

There continues to be an increasing overlap between the commodities and securities markets. For example, stock index futures have for a long time been traded in the commodities markets subject to the jurisdiction of the Commodity Futures Trading Commission (CFTC). In 2000, Congress enacted the Commodity Futures Modernization Act (CFMA) (Pub. Law 106–554 (Dec. 21, 2001)), which further increased the competition between the securities and commodities markets by permitting futures on individual securities and subjecting them to regulation by the CFTC. One consequence of the increased competition in securities-related investments between the commodities and securities markets is that broker-dealers may be subject to regulation by both the SEC and the CFTC. The CFMA mandates that the two agencies coordinate and eliminate duplicative regulation over broker dealers.

b. *Registration of Foreign Broker–Dealers*

1934 Act § 15(a)(1) requires registration of foreign broker-dealers who utilize the mails or other means of interstate commerce to effect transactions in nonexempt securities. "Interstate commerce" is defined to include commerce between a foreign country and any state. 1934 Act § 30(b) relieves foreign brokers from the broker-dealer registration requirements imposed by § 15, provided that the foreign broker is operating outside of the jurisdiction of the United States.

The Commission has stated it would take no action to require registration of a foreign broker who sold foreign securities to American investors solely through registered American brokers because the Americans would be protected by the registration of the American brokers. Further, even though it has the authority to do so,the Commission has not insisted upon registration of foreign brokers who use the mails or interstate commerce to buy shares in mutual funds in the United States for sale abroad.

1934 Act Rule 15a–6 clarifies the SEC's stance on foreign broker-dealer registration requirements. The Commission Rule exempts certain foreign brokers or dealers who would normally be subject to § 15(a) registration requirements because of attempts to induce the purchase or sale of any security by a United States person. The rule provides an exemption in a number of situations. First, the rule exempts transactions by a foreign broker or dealer with or for persons that have not been solicited by the foreign broker. Second, there is an exemption for certain transactions by foreign brokers or dealers on behalf of major United States institutional investors. The rule also provides an exemption for transactions by a foreign broker or dealer with or for: (i) a registered domestic broker-dealer or a bank acting as a broker-dealer as permitted by United States law; (ii) various enumerated foreign banking agencies, including the United Nations; (iii) a foreign person temporarily residing in the United States, provided that the foreign broker had a preexisting relationship with such foreign person; (iv) any transaction with a United States person residing permanently outside the United States, provided that the transactions take place outside of the United States; and (v) United States citizens residing abroad, provided that the transactions take place outside the United States and that the foreign broker or dealer does not direct its selling efforts toward identifiable groups of American citizens residing abroad.

c. *Registration of Over-the-Counter Derivative Dealers—"Broker–Dealer Lite"*

Many firms that do not otherwise engage in securities transactions requiring registration as a broker-dealer have moved their derivative business to offshore subsidiaries in order to avoid SEC registration for domestic activities. In order to stop this flight abroad, the SEC adopted a less onerous registration for firms engaging only in over-the-counter derivatives whose customers are persons with more than ten million dollars in assets. This less onerous registration requirement is known as "broker-dealer lite." 1934 Act Rule 3b–15 permits OTC derivatives dealers to engage in limited securities-related activities. OTC derivative dealers are exempt from broker-dealer registration, however, they are required to set up a system of internal controls to monitor and manage the risks arising out of their derivatives activities. There has not been a great rush to take advantage of broker-dealer lite. As of March 2001, there was only one broker-dealer lite registration. One SEC official indicated that he would not expect more than ten or twelve registrations.As of January 2010 there were fifteen OTC derivatives dealers registrants. See http://www.risk.net/risk-magazine/news/1586034/number-otc-derivatives-dealers-double-us-reforms. Furthermore, it was projected that the number could double in light of pending financial reform. Id.

d. *Regulation of Swap Dealers and Major Swap Participants*

The Dodd–Frank Wall Street Reform and Consumer Protection Act of 2010, created two new categories of professionals that must be registered under the Securities Exchange Act. (Pub.Law 111–203, H.R. 4173 (111th Cong. 2d sess. 2010)). Those two new categories are (1) security-based swap dealers and (2) major security-based swap participants. A "security-based swap dealer" is defined as a person who (i) holds itself out as a dealer in security-based swaps, or (ii) makes a market in security-based swaps, or (iii) regularly enters into swaps with counterparties as an ordinary course of business for its own account, or (iv) engages in activity commonly known in the trade as a dealer or market maker in security-based swaps. 1934 Act § 3(a)(71). The full scope of a "major security-based swap participant" will not be known until implementing regulations are adopted but the thrust of the status is a person other than a security-based swap dealer that maintains a substantial (to be defined) non-hedging position in security-based swaps giving rise to substantial counterparty exposure that could impact the economy systemically. Security-based swap dealers and major swap participants that must register under the Exchange Act are made subject to a variety of burdensome duties, including capital and margin requirements, extensive reporting and recordkeeping, business conduct standards, disclosure duties, risk management obligations, and many other operational mandates. The specifics and implementation of the regulation will be unveiled by SEC rulemaking. The Dodd–Frank's mandates for security-based swaps parallel the mandate to the CFTC for all other swaps.

§ 21. Definitions of Broker and Dealer

Broker is defined in 1934 Act § 3(a)(4)(A) to include any person, other than a bank, in the business of buying and selling securities for others. To fall within the definition, it is not necessary that the broker deal directly with customers; thus, for example, clearing brokers specialists on an exchange are subject to SEC regulation. A dealer is defined by 1934 Act § 3(a)(5)(A) to be any person other than a bank who is in the business of purchasing securities for his or her own account.

The Act's registration requirements, as well as the definitions of broker and dealer, are drafted broadly to include a wide range of securities professionals. Key terminology in the definitions of broker and dealer is the phrase "engaged in the business." Merely providing information that may facilitate investors does not classify the provider as a broker-dealer. Thus, for example, providing information over the Internet does not in itself trigger the definition of broker or dealer.

In deciding whether a firm is acting as a broker-dealer, a number of factors are considered, including whether the firm (1) receives transaction-based compensation, such as commissions or referral fees, (2) is involved in negotiations between an issuer of securities and investors, (3) makes valuations as to the merits of the investment or gives advice, and (4) is active rather than passive in locating investors. For example, participating in a public offering as an underwriter or dealer requires 1934 Act registration as a broker-dealer. A service purportedly seeking to facilitate communications between registered broker-dealers that invites investors to participate through their broker-dealers is sufficiently engaged in soliciting retail customers so as to implicate the broker-dealer registration requirements, especially where fees would be based on a per order basis. See

BondGlobe, 2001 WL 103418 (SEC No Action Letter Feb. 6, 2001). This is the type of active participation in securities transactions that distinguishes the operation from one passively providing an Internet portal between investors and registered broker-dealers. See id.; Charles Schwab & Co., Inc., 1996 WL 762999 (SEC No Action Letter November 27, 1996) (granting no action relief to Internet providers to provide a link between their subscribers and a registered broker-dealer).

Regularity of participation is a primary indication of being "engaged in the business" and therefore of acting as a broker-dealer. Participation in securities transactions, participation in securities transactions "at key points in the chain of distribution" is considered to be acting as a broker-dealer. E.g., Massachusetts Financial Services, Inc. v. Securities Investor Protection Corp., 411 F.Supp. 411, 415 (D.Mass.), aff'd, 545 F.2d 754 (1st Cir. 1976), cert. denied, 431 U.S. 904 (1977); BD Advantage, Inc., 2000 WL 1742088 (SEC No Action Letter Oct. 11, 2000).

Participation in securities transactions that can qualify as engaging in the business as a broker-dealer include selecting the market to which a securities transaction will be sent, assisting an issuer to structure prospective securities transactions, helping an issuer identify potential purchasers of securities, soliciting securities transactions (including advertising), and participating in the order-taking or order-routing process (for example, by taking transaction orders from customers). "Factors indicating that a person is 'engaged in the business' include, among others: receiving transaction-related compensation; holding one's self out as a broker, as executing trades, or as assisting others in completing securities transactions; and participating in the securities business with some degree of regularity. In addition to indicating that a person is 'effecting transactions,' soliciting securities transactions is also evidence of being 'engaged in the business.'" BD Advantage, Inc., 2000 WL 1742088 (SEC No Action Letter Oct. 11, 2000).

Being engaged in the securities business does not mean that a company must have that business as its sole or even primary business. An individual advertising on a single, isolated basis an interest to engage in securities transactions for his or her own account might not be "engaged in the business," but more frequent advertising could cause that individual to be engaged in the business.

In interpreting the dealer registration requirements generally, the SEC has made a distinction between traders who are acting primarily for themselves and dealers who transact business for others. As explained by the SEC, the registration provisions have been applied to dealers, which includes those firms that normally have a regular clientele, hold themselves out as buying or selling securities at a regular place of business, have a regular turnover of inventory (or participate in the sale or distribution of new issues, such as by acting as an underwriter). In contrast, traders who deal exclusively for their

own account will not have to be registered as broker-dealers.

§ 22.　Exclusion for Banks but Not Subsidiar-
ies; Regulation R

Banks are excluded from the definition of broker
and dealer and hence cannot be registered as broker-dealers under the 1934 Act. 1934 Act §§ 3(a)(4),
3(a)(5). The exclusion does not include subsidiaries
of banks that engage in securities transactions. Initially, the Glass–Steagall Act of 1933 kept banks out
of the commercial securities business because of the
restrictions it placed on such activity. However, in
the 1980s, bank involvement in customer securities
transactions began to expand as banks, through
subsidiaries, started acting as discount brokers and
began soliciting brokerage customers from the general public. In 1999 when Congress enacted the
Graham–Leach–Bliley Act (GLBA) and repealed the
Glass–Steagall Act it enacted a system of functional
regulation. Subsidiaries of banks can engage in all
sorts of securities related activities and their activities are subject to SEC control. Similarly, financial
holding companies can engage in banking, securities, and insurance activities and their securities
activities are regulated by the SEC.

The GLBA adopted two categories of activities
that would be exempt from broker-dealer registration under the Securities Exchange Act of 1934.
These two types of activities are bank securities
activities that relate to functions traditionally performed by banks and transactions that relate to

traditional bank products. The banking exemptions from broker-dealer regulation for traditional banking activities include such things as trust activities (unless the bank customer has discretionary trading authority), stock purchase plans, sweep accounts, private securities placements, and municipal securities.

Regulation R

After many years of proposed and temporary rulemaking the SEC and Federal Reserve Board adopted Regulation R to clarify when banking activities will implicate the securities broker-dealer registration requirements. Regulation R embodies what have become known as the "push out" provisions. A bank can "push out" its securities activities to an SEC regulated subsidiary and retain activities in the banking enterprise. Regulation R (17 C.F.R. § 247.___) contains specific exceptions with respect to certain securities-related activities that banks may engage in without being considered securities broker-dealers. Regulation R thus helps a bank determine which securities-related activities need to be pushed out of the banking operations.

Among other things, Regulation R adds clarity to the statutory requirement that banks may perform only "clerical or ministerial functions" with respect to securities brokerage transactions and that representatives of a bank may receive only a "nominal, one-time cash fee of a fixed dollar amount" for referring a bank customer to a securities broker-dealer and the fee may not be contingent on actual transactions. Regulation R exempts from the limitations on referral fees with respect to referrals of institutional and high net worth investors, provided that the broker-dealer performs a suitability or sophistication analysis of the customer.Regulation R Rule 700. Regulation R further provides clarification of the bank exception from broker-dealer registration for banks acting as a trustee or fiduciary as part of the banking services as well as for the exceptions for sweep accounts and for custodial and safekeeping accounts that are offered as part of their banking services. Regulation R Rules 721, 722, 740, 741, 760.

§ 23. Exemptions

a. Dealers of Exempt Securities

There are exemptions from the broker-dealer registration requirements. Persons who effect transactions *solely* in exempt securities are not subject to the Act's broker-dealer registration requirements. 1934 Act § 15(a)(1). Exempted securities include: government and municipal securities, interest in a trust fund administered by a bank, interest in an insurance policy, and securities with a primarily intrastate market. However, for example, in the case of municipal and government securities dealers, broker-dealers will be subject to other regulatory requirements.

b. Intrastate Exemption

As mentioned above, broker-dealers whose business is exclusively intrastate are exempt from registration. All of a broker's transactions must be intrastate in order to be eligible for the exemption. One out of state transaction can negate the exemption. Even if all transactions are intrastate, either present or previous interstate business affiliations may take a broker-dealer out of intrastate exemption. For a transaction to be included within the category of "intrastate," all phases of the transaction must take place intrastate. Thus, for example, in Guon v. United States, 285 F.2d 140, 144 (8th Cir.1960), the intrastate requirement was not satisfied when a broker negotiated and agreed upon a sale of securities within one state, but received payment for the securities from a second state.

c. OTC Derivatives Dealers

Broker-dealers whose exclusive business consists of dealing in securities that fall within the category of "eligible OTC derivative instruments," as defined in 1934 Act Rule 3b–13, qualify as over-the-counter derivatives dealers. These OTC derivatives dealers qualify for a short-form registration known as "broker-dealer lite" so long as their business continues to be limited to qualifying OTC derivate instruments. See § 20 supra.

d. Investment Advisers and Financial Consultants

Investment advisers also often seek exemption from broker-dealer registration. Registration as a broker-dealer will be required if the investment adviser: (1) executes transactions for its clients; (2) charges fees based upon the amount of securities transactions effected by its clients; or (3) takes possession of its clients' funds or securities. Broker-dealers who offer advisory services, including asset-based rather than transaction-based fees will have to register as investment advisers under the IAA in addition to their broker-dealer registration. See, e.g., Goldstein v. SEC, 451 F.3d 873 (D.C. Cir. 2006).

Financial services consultants, who provide issuers with advice and assistance in preparing offerings of securities, historically have not been required to register as broker-dealers so long as their activities do not include certain identifying aspects of broker-dealer status. Activities found by the staff not to show broker-dealer status are: (1) determining and giving advice on applicable law; (2) advising upon anti-fraud concerns; (3) advising an issuer on its financial potential and recommending methods of financing; (4) advising upon and preparing appropriate disclosure documents and clearing them with appropriate government agencies; (5) providing appropriate debt instruments; (6) advising the issuer as to necessary charter amendments; (7) making arrangements with a bank for retiring debt instruments and payment of principal and interest; (8) advising an issuer about clerical work involved in selling bonds; (9) suggesting to an issuer procedures for selling bonds; (10) suggesting a date of sale; and (11) suggesting investment opportunities for temporarily idle proceeds of an offering.

e. *Registered Representatives*

Broker-dealer employees engaged in sales activities are generally required to be registered representatives. Registered representatives associated with a registered broker-dealer ordinarily will be exempt from registration as a broker-dealer. As such, the registered representative will qualify as a person associated with the broker-dealer rather than a broker-dealer in his or her own right. However, the exemption will not be available when the registered representative is conducting business on his or her own. See Roth v. SEC, 22 F.3d 1108 (D.C. Cir. 1994).

The exemption from registration as a broker-dealer does not insulate registered representatives and other associated persons from SEC regulation. Thus, for example, employees of brokerage firms who have regular contact with the public and act as order takers have to qualify as registered representatives. Exchange Services, Inc. v. SEC, 797 F.2d 188 (4th Cir. 1986). Furthermore, associated persons who do not have to register nevertheless are still subject to the SEC's disciplinary authority. Haberman v. SEC, 205 F.3d 1345 (8th Cir. 2000).

f. *Insurance Products Dealers*

Dealers transacting business solely in insurance products are generally exempt from the broker-dealer registration requirements. Thus, licensed insurance companies, which through insurance agents and registered broker-dealers offer life insurance products which qualify as securities, need not register as broker-dealers. *See* 1934 Act § 3(a)(12).

g. *Finders*

Also exempt from broker-dealer registration requirements are independent business persons whose role is to find buyers and sellers of securities, and who do not themselves engage in the purchase and sale of securities but offer their services to aid customers in seeking business. For example, these "finders" or "channelers" may be in the business of identifying companies suitable for merger, or merely of directing customers to brokers and dealers, or in locating investors for a business seeking to raise capital. The registration exception for finders is premised on the judgment that finders who do not effect securities transactions for others are not truly dealing in securities and thus need not be registered to protect the public interest.

However, it is not always easy to determine whether a finder's activities would require broker-dealer registration. In deciding whether a particular finder is "effecting" transactions for others and thus needs to register, the SEC staff may ask whether the finder (1) was involved in negotiations for the sale of the securities; (2) discussed details of the nature of the securities sold or made any recommendations; (3) was compensated on a commission basis linked to sales; or (4) was previously involved in the sales of securities. The SEC takes a narrow view of the registration exception for finders. Nevertheless, where a finder's activity consists of nothing more than bringing entities together and does not participate in further negotiations, absent unusual circumstances, this activity will not categorize the finder as a broker-dealer. However, where the finder does more than bring the parties together, the involvement in the transaction is likely to result in a finding of broker-dealer activity that requires registration under the 1934 Act.

h. Certain Persons Associated With the Issuer

Officers, directors, and employees of a securities issuer who participate in a distribution of the issuer's securities are not deemed to be broker-dealers if they fall within 1934 Act Rule 3a4–1's safe harbor provisions. The safe harbor is dependent upon both the nature of the associated person's activities and the nature of the securities being offered. The SEC release adopting Rule 3a4–1 advised that the rule "does provide legal certainty to those persons whose activities meet the conditions of the rule," but that adherence to the rule is not the exclusive means for persons associated with an issuer to be exempted from broker-dealer registration. Sec. Exch. Act Rel. No. 34–22172, [1984 Transfer Binder] Fed.Sec.L.Rep. (CCH) ¶ 83,792 (June 27, 1985).

To be eligible for 1934 Act Rule 3a4–1's safe harbor, associated persons of an issuer must satisfy three preliminary conditions; the associated person cannot be (1) subject to statutory disqualification as defined in 1934 Act § 3(a)(39), (2) paid commissions based upon sales; or (3) associated with a broker-dealer.

If the foregoing preliminary conditions are met, the associated person must comply with one of three alternative restrictions on activities to reach the safe harbor. First, the associated person can limit his or her sales efforts to certain specified activities which do not appear to require the protection that broker-dealer registration provides. Those specified activities include: (1) sales made only to financial institutions and intermediaries; (2) sales of exempted securities under 1933 Act §§ 3(a)(7), 3(a)(9), or 3(a)(10) in connection with certain reorganizations and exchanges; (3) sales made in connection with reorganizations; (4) transactions involving securities are issued to shareholders pursuant to a plan adopted by a shareholder vote; or (5) transactions involving securities are issued pursuant to an employee benefit plan. As a second alternative, the associated person may sell the issuer's securities, but must (1) also perform substantial duties for the issuer other than selling securities; (2) not be or have been within the past twelve months a broker, a dealer, or an associated person of a broker, dealer, or investment advisor; and (3) not participate in the sale of securities for any issuer more than once every twelve months. The third alternative allows the associated person to make sales for an issuer, but only if that associated person's involvement in the sales is passive. Under this alternative a seller can only communicate in writing with prospective purchasers when responding to inquiries initiated by potential purchasers and the written communication must be approved by a partner, an officer, or a director of the issuer. Communications in the form of "cold calls" are not allowed. 1934 Act Rule 3a4–1. Response to inquiries of potential purchasers must be limited to information contained in a registration statement or other offering document. In addition, the associated person can perform ministerial and clerical work, such as bookkeeping entries and arranging for the delivery of securities.

i. *SEC's General Exemptive Authority*

In 1996, Congress gave the Commission general exemptive authority that can be exercised either by rulemaking or exemptive order. 1934 Act § 36. Thus, the SEC has exemptive authority beyond the statutes and rules discussed above. The only limitation is that the exemption be in the public interest and not inconsistent with investor protection.

§ 24. FINRA Registration for Certain Associated Persons

As discussed directly above, the SEC registration generally applies to firms rather than individuals. The SROs extend their registration requirements to many individuals associated with registered broker-dealer firms. These individuals are subject to qualification and registration with FINRA (formerly the NASD). For example, in order to be what we commonly think of as a stock broker, a customer representative, or an account executive, an individual must be registered with FINRA as a registered representative. In order to qualify as a registered representative, an individual must have a sponsoring broker-dealer. An applicant seeking qualification as a registered representative must fill out a Form U–4, which details the applicant's employment history including any past violations of securities laws and regulations or other laws. Many state regulators have a comparable form for registered representatives doing business within the state. After filling out an application and the required Form U–4, the applicant must then take a qualifying exam administered by FINRA. There is also a qualifying exam for registration in states where the registered representative will be conducting business. The Series 7 examination is the exam that qualifies the applicant to serve in a wide variety of capacities as a registered representative. Associated persons can also obtain more restricted registrations that limit the activities in which the registered representative may engage.

An owner of a broker-dealer firm or a branch office must qualify for registration as a principal. As is the case with registered representative registration, registered principals must first qualify as principals through an application and examination process. The chief compliance officer of a registered broker-dealer must be registered with FINRA as a principal. A complete list of the registration categories can be found on the FINRA website (http://www.finra.org/Industry/Compliance/Registra tion/QualificationsExams/RegisteredReps/Brochure/ P009865).

Once an individual qualifies as a registered representative or is otherwise registered with FINRA, he or she is subject to continuous regulatory oversight. Registered associated persons are also subject to continuing education and ethics requirements. Registered representatives must also report regulatory violations and customer complaints to FINRA. It is possible to look up a registered representative's disciplinary history (see http://www.finra.org/ Investors/ToolsCalculators/BrokerCheck/index.htm).

As this Nutshell went to press, FINRA had proposed adding registration requirements for broker-dealer back office personnel. As mentioned earlier, the back office personnel who would have to register include those responsible for development and approval of valuation models, employees who manage trade confirmations, account statements, trade settlement, and margin accounts, as well as employees who oversee stock loans, securities lending, prime brokerage, receipt and delivery of securities and those involved with financial or regulatory reporting. See FINRA Reg. Notice 10–25, Registration and Qualification of Certain Operations Personnel, http://www.finra.org/web/groups/industry/@ip/@reg /@notice/documents/notices/p121533.pdf (May 2010).

§ 25. Net Capital and Reserve Requirements

The solvency of broker-dealers has long been a concern of policy makers. As discussed in § 72 infra, in 1970 Congress enacted the Securities Investor Protection Act to provide for customers' insurance against losses due to brokerage firm insolvency. However, other protections trying to prevent such insolvencies have been in place much longer. The SEC has for a long time imposed net capital requirements on broker-dealer firms. A companion

set of requirements is found in the reserve requirements. Both of these are discussed briefly below.

a. Net Capital Requirements

In 1942, the SEC adopted its net capital rule,
which is designed to assure a safe balance between
a brokerage firm's securities holdings, cash, and
liabilities. Sec. Exch. Act Rel. No. 34–3323 (SEC
Oct. 29, 1942). The current net capital rule imposes
extremely complicated accounting and solvency requirements for a brokerage firm's assets and liabilities. 1934 Act Rule 15c3–1.

The basic financial responsibility standards for
broker-dealers are found in the "net capital" rules
adopted by the SEC under authority of 1934 Act
§ 15(c)(3). Prior to the financial debacle suffered by
the securities industry from 1968 to 1970, securities
firms belonging to exchanges that had "net capital"
rules deemed to be more stringent than those of the
SEC were exempt from the SEC's requirements.
However, after SEC and Congressional investigations showed how flexibly the exchanges had interpreted their rules to allow member firms to continue in business with inadequate capital, the SEC
revoked this exemption and made all broker-dealers
subject to its requirements.

Under 1934 Act Rule 15c3–1, a broker-dealer
must maintain "net capital" of at least $250,000.
"Net capital" is defined as "net worth" (excess of
assets over liabilities), subject to many special adjustments prescribed in the rule. One of the more
important special adjustments is the "haircut" or

discount that must be applied in valuing securities listed on the asset side of the balance sheet. The net capital rule requires that securities be discounted by a specified amount; this amount varies depending on the type of security. The haircut is designed to provide an additional margin of safety in light of the volatility of securities prices.

In addition to the net worth test, a broker-dealer may not let its aggregate indebtedness exceed 1500% of its net capital (800% during its first year of business). A broker-dealer can alternatively qualify under Rule 15c3–1(f), which is designed to test its general financial integrity and liquidity and its ability to meet its continuing commitments to its customers.

b.   Customers' Funds and Securities: The Customer Protection Rule and the Reserve Requirements

Customers leave large amounts of cash and securities with their brokers. Securities held by broker-dealers are of two types: securities purchased "on margin" (see § 26 infra) (i.e., with the broker advancing part of the purchase price to the customer), which (under the standard margin agreement) the broker is entitled to hold as security for the loan and to repledge to secure its own borrowings; and "fully-paid" securities, which the broker holds solely as a convenience for the customer and is supposed to "segregate" from the broker's own securities. 1934 Act Rule 15c2–1(a). Cash held by brokers, called "free credit balances" arise principally from two sources: a deposit of cash by a customer prior to giving his broker a purchase order, and receipt by the broker of proceeds of a sale of securities, or interest of dividend income, which has not yet been reinvested or delivered to the customer.

With respect to fully-paid securities, investigators of the securities industry's operational crises in 1968–1970 discovered that many firms had lost control of their records and did not have in their possession many of the securities that they were supposed to be holding as custodians for their customers. Accordingly, the SEC in 1972 adopted 1934 Act Rule 15c3–3, which requires that all brokers "promptly obtain and ... thereafter maintain the physical possession or control of all fully-paid securities," and prescribes daily determinations of compliance with the rule.

With respect to cash free credit balances, brokers have traditionally mingled the cash belonging to customers with their own assets used in their business. Since 1964, 1934 Act Rule 15c3–2 has required brokers to notify their customers at least quarterly that such funds (a) are not segregated and may be used in the business, and (b) are payable to the customer on demand. In the wake of the debacles in the late 1960s, which revealed that many firms had been using customers' free credit balances as their own working capital, there were demands for complete segregation of these cash balances. The industry argued, however, that it should continue to have interest-free use of these moneys to finance customer-related transactions (principally margin loans). The result was 1934 Act Rule 15c3–3, adopted by the SEC in 1972, which requires each broker to maintain a "Special Reserve Bank Account for the Exclusive Benefit of Customers" in which it holds cash or U.S. government securities in an amount equal to (a) free credit balances in customers' accounts (plus other amounts owing to customers) less (b) debit balances in customers' cash and margin accounts. Violations of the customer protection rule can result in revocation of a broker-dealer's registration.

§ 26. The Margin Rules and Extension of Credit

a. *Margin Transactions Explained*

Not all securities are purchased in a straight cash transaction. A large number of securities transactions, especially those by speculative investors, are entered into by the broker extending credit to the purchaser while the lender holds the purchased securities as collateral. Securities purchases on credit are referred to as margin transactions. A margin purchase gives the security holder leverage. Leverage allows an investor to take an investment positions with a lower upfront payment, carrying the rest of the purchase price on credit. Thus while significantly increasing the risk of investment, leverage obtained through a purchase on margin also increases the potential gain. Excessive credit balances create undue investor risk. In addition, brokerage firms that extended high levels of credit in the 1920s were wiped out by the stock market crash of 1929. The margin requirements were designed to curb such excesses.

The effect of price changes on a margin account can be understood from examining how an increase in the loan value of a securities account will increase the likelihood of a margin call. Assume that an investor has a stock portfolio consisting entirely of marginable securities with a current market value of $100,000; the risk of a margin maintenance call is greatly reduced the less the investor borrows against his or her portfolio. For example, if the investor borrows thirty percent of the value of stocks (i.e. $30,000), the stocks would have to decline in value by more than fifty-seven percent before the investor would be subject to a maintenance call, assuming a margin maintenance requirement of thirty percent imposed by the investor's brokerage firm. The following table demonstrates the effects of margin borrowing against $100,000 worth of stock:

If investor borrows:		A maintenance call will be issued if the portfolio value declines to:	Percentage decline before maintenance call occurs:
$50,000	(50%)	$71,429	29%
$40,000	(40%)	$57,143	43%
$30,000	(30%)	$42,857	57%
$20,000	(20%)	$28,571	71%

$10,000   (10%) $14,286   85%

The examples that follow demonstrate the calculation of permissible margin levels for an initial purchase of securities. If an investor wants to buy 10,000 shares of ABC Corp. stock, which is trading at $10 per share (for a total $100,000 for 10,000 shares), and wants to make the purchase with only $75,000 cash, he or she can do so by borrowing the remaining $25,000 that is necessary to complete the purchase. The margin calculation for the account would be as follows:

The investor purchases 10,000 shares of ABC Corp. at $10 per share for a total cost of $100,000. The investor would then deposit the $75,000 cash with the broker and borrow the remaining $25,000 from the broker.

$100,000 (value of stock) − ($25,000) (debit balance) = $75,000 (net equity)

$75,000 (net equity) ÷ $100,000 (value of stock) = 75% net equity = 25% credit balance = 75% margin

The next example demonstrates the calculation of the maximum loan permitted under the Federal Reserve Board's fifty percent limit under its margin rules for the extension of credit. An investor wants to purchase 10,000 shares of ABC Corp. stock, which is trading at $10 per share (a total of $100,000 for the 10,000 shares). The investor can purchase on fifty percent margin by purchasing the

stock for $100,000, using $50,000 cash and borrowing $50,000 from the broker:

  10,000 shares ABC Corp. @ $10 = $100,000 total
  equity

  $50,000 cash + $50,000 margin loan

This is the maximum that the investor may purchase with $50,000 cash since it puts the investor at
the Federal Reserve Board's fifty percent margin
limit for the extension of credit. Each time an
investor purchases additional securities on margin,
it is considered another extension of credit so that
the 50% maximum credit balance (or minimum fifty
percent margin) will apply to each purchase. Thus,
for example, after making the first purchase of the
10,000 ABC Corp. shares, if the investor now wants
to purchase an additional $10,000 of stock he or she
must deposit at least an additional $5,000 cash (or
at least an additional $10,000 worth of other mar-
ginable collateral) in order to make the second
purchase.

  Separate from the limits put on the initial extension of credit are margin maintenance requirements. These requirements relate to the potential
increase of an investor's credit balance due to a
decrease in value of the securities he holds and/or
interest charged on the loan/credit balance. The
following are examples of the operation of the margin maintenance requirements of at least twenty-
five percent that are imposed by the SROs:

  An investor's securities account has a $50,000
  debit on which the investor will be charged inter-

est by the lending brokerage firm. The interest on the investor's debt will in turn be added to the account's debit balance. For example, if the $10 per share price of the 10,000 shares of ABC Corp. stock remains constant, assuming 6% interest (1/2% per month), after one month the investor's account would incur an additional $250 debit. The investor's account would still consist of 10,-000 shares ABC Corp. at $10 per share for a total of $100,000. There would be the initial $50,000 debit plus an additional $250 resulting from the interest charged over the first month. This would result in a total debit balance of $50,250. The margin computation would then be as follows:

$100,000 (value of stock) − $50,250 (debit balance) = $49,750 (net equity)

$49,750 (net equity) ÷ $100,000 (value of stock) = 49.75% margin

The foregoing example would be in compliance with the SRO margin maintenance requirements, but not with the Federal Reserve Board's extension of credit requirements of 50% if this had occurred in coincidence with a purchase of additional securities. Assume that after the first month, the price of ABC Corp. has dropped to $8 per share. The investor's account would then consist of 10,000 shares of ABC Corp. at $8 per share for a total of $80,000. The account would have the $50,000 initial debit plus the $250 interest for a total debit balance of $50,250. The account would still be in compliance with the minimum margin maintenance requirement:

$80,000 (value of stock) − $50,250 (debit balance) = $29,750 (net equity)

$29,750 (net equity) ÷ $80,000 (value of stock) = 37.1875% margin

However, if during the first month the price of ABC has dropped to $6 (instead of the $8 per share in the previous example), then the investor's account would be computed as follows. There would be 10,000 shares of ABC Corp. at $6 per share for a total of $60,000. The account would have the $50,000 initial debit plus the $250 interest for a total debit balance of $50,025. The account would not be in compliance with the minimum margin maintenance requirement:

$60,000 (value of stock) − $50,250 (debit balance) = $9,750 (net equity)

$9,750 (net equity) ÷ $60,000 (value of stock) = 16.25% margin

This example results in a total that is below the NYSE, AMEX, & NASDAQ minimum margin maintenance requirements and the investor would be subject to a margin call. Either additional collateral would have to be supplied or the securities in the account would be liquidated to pay off the debit balance.

b.   Limitations on the Extension of Credit for Securities Transactions

1934 Act § 7 sets out a complex system of regulation with regard to the extension of credit for securities transactions, but does not apply to exempt securities. 1934 Act § 7(a) delegates to the Federal Reserve Board the authority to promulgate rules governing the extension of credit where securities are used as collateral to secure the loan. Various regulations have been adopted with regard to broker-dealers, banks, and other persons extending credit in this manner. Broker-dealer margin rule enforcement lies with the SEC through injunctions, criminal proceedings, revocation of registration, or suspension from membership in self-regulatory organizations. In 1996, Congress preempted the states' ability to regulate the extension of credit in securities transactions. 1934 Act 8(a). As pointed out below, the credit extension rules are not limited to traditional margin accounts. The rules also apply to late payments in cash accounts.

Under 1934 Act § 7, the initial extension of credit may not be for an amount greater than the higher of (1) fifty-five percent of the security's then current market price or (2) one hundred percent of the lowest market price of the security during the preceding thirty-six calendar months but no more than seventy-five percent of the current market price. Certain exempt governmental securities are allowed to trade with a much higher margin. This more highly leveraged transaction for federal government notes is more in line with the margin requirements for the more speculative commodity markets. Notwithstanding the statutory fifty-five percent ceiling on credit, the Federal Reserve Board has imposed an even lower credit ceiling of fifty percent. Reg. T, 12 C.F.R. § 220.18.

The applicable rules of the Federal Reserve Board for broker-dealers' extension of credit are found in Regulation T. Regulation U governs bank loans that are secured directly or indirectly by stock or other marginable securities. Regulation X applies to margin borrowing by residents of the United States of either domestic or foreign lenders. Regulation X prohibits borrowers from entering into transactions that would violate Regulations T, or U.

In order to qualify for an extension of credit under Regulation T, the securities must either be traded on a national securities exchange or be actively traded in the over-the-counter market. The Federal Reserve Board now provides for the automatic marginability of stocks that are part of the NASDAQ System. Additionally, foreign sovereign debt securities are marginable to the extent of their "good faith" loan value.

As noted above, the margin rules are not limited to accounts authorized for margin transactions. Accounts not authorized for margin transactions are considered to be cash accounts. The margin rules require that whenever a security is purchased in a cash account, payment must be made within a specified settlement period after the date of purchase or else the broker-dealer must cancel or otherwise liquidate the transaction.

In mid–1993, the settlement period for most securities was shortened from five to three business days. The settlement date for options remains the business day following the transaction. A broker's delay in liquidating the account will not relieve the customer of the obligation to pay for the securities.

c. *Margin Maintenance Requirements*

The statutory (and Federal Reserve Board) limits on margin accounts apply only to the *initial* extension of credit and do not deal with an increase in the ratio of the debit of the margin account in relation to the value of the securities due to a subsequent decline in the price of securities used as collateral. In other words, under both SEC and Federal Reserve Board regulation it lies purely within the lender's discretion to decide at what point additional securities as collateral or cash will be needed to fortify a margin account where the value of the current collateral is declining. However, the exchanges and NASDAQ impose margin maintenance requirements. Under these margin maintenance rules, the current market value of the collateral must be at least twenty-five percent of the account's total value. Thus, there are minimum margin maintenance requirements for all accounts. Generally, brokerage firms assure compliance with the margin maintenance requirements by instituting an internal policy for "house calls" at a level above the regulatory minimum. The higher house call level thus provides a safety zone in the event that the market is unusually volatile or the customer delays in providing the necessary additional collateral.

A "margin call" whereby the customer is required to come up with additional collateral lest the margined securities be sold, will never be required by operation of law unless a new security is purchased for the account. This is thus left to the broker-dealer's discretion and the twenty-five percent minimum required by FINRA, the exchanges, and by NASDAQ. Most brokerage firms have established their own policies for margin calls, many of which are more stringent than the FINRA, NASDAQ, and exchange rules. Brokers' guidelines may also depend in part not only upon the value of the collateral but also on the diversification of the margined securities as well as their reliability.

d. Margin Disclosure Requirements; Suitability

In addition to the substantive margin regulation set forth in the Federal Reserve Board and SRO organization regulations, margin accounts trigger special disclosure obligations. See FINRA Conduct Rule 2264 (formerly NASD Conduct Rule 2341). The customer must be given a margin disclosure statement when the margin account is opened and must also receive a disclosure statement annually. The disclosure statement is designed to alert customers to the risks associated with margin accounts. The required disclosure at the opening of a margin account is designed to inform the customer of margin-related risks. The annual disclosure requirement is designed to remind the customer of these risks.

By themselves, margin trades are high risk trans-actions. The advent of online trading and increased market volatility can heighten those risks.

Failure to fully inform the client of margin risks can result in liability for losses caused as a result thereof. However, when a customer understands the nature of margin risks, he or she will not be able to state a claim for relief.

In addition to the foregoing disclosure require-ments, 1934 Act Rule 10b–16 requires broker-deal-ers to adequately disclose to the customer the cost of any securities transaction where credit is extend-ed. The disclosure obligations imposed by SEC Rule 10b–16 are supplemented not only by Reg. T but also by 1934 Act Rule 15c2–5, which imposes disclo-sure requirements for certain loans and extensions of credit by broker-dealers in connection with secu-rities transactions.

The risks associated with margin accounts are such that margin transactions are not suitable for all investors. A broker who uses margin trading in violation of the suitability requirements has violat-ed broker-dealer conduct rules. (See § 56 infra).

e. *Remedies for Violations of the Margin Rules*

At one time, some courts recognized a private remedy in the hands of the customer who is injured by violation of the credit extension rules. However, the overwhelming majority of more recent decisions is to the contrary. E.g. Useden v. Acker, 947 F.2d 1563 (11th Cir. 1991). The absence of an implied remedy under the margin rules is bolstered by the amendment to 1934 Act § 7(f) and ensuing Federal Reserve Board Reg. X rendering the customer himself or herself in violation of the Act.

§ 27. A Brokerage Firm's Duty to Supervise

a. *Duty to Supervise*

Brokerage firms have an obligation to supervise their personnel. Cases involving a brokerage firm's alleged failure to supervise can be highly factual in nature. However, some generalizations can be made. Guidance as to what constitutes proper supervision of a firm's employees can be gleaned from the cases, as well as the SEC and SRO decisions. The duty to supervise starts with a firm's president, who may delegate some supervisory authority to others. For example, within a branch office, the branch manager has a duty to supervise.

The duty to supervise is not limited to personnel with an official supervisory title. If, in fact, someone within the firm has actual supervisory authority over a violator of the securities laws, the supervisor can be held accountable for the violations. A firm's supervision activities should be overseen by the firm's compliance department.

The key supervision duties, which are generally performed by a firm's branch manager, include (1) having familiarity with the branch office's clients and accounts; (2) performing daily reviews of order tickets, making sure that the tickets were completed properly; (3) supervising active accounts monthly and making inquiries into any unusual activities; (4) completing logs of the supervisory activities that were performed; and (5) forwarding documentation of the supervisory reviews to the firm's compliance department.

The extent of the duty to supervise will depend on the facts of any given case and will vary to the extent that any "red flags" have been raised. Thus, a firm's discovery of problem brokers or other unusual activity triggers a heightened duty to supervise. Therefore, it is crucial for branch managers and other supervisory personnel to be on the lookout for red flags that could trigger this heightened supervisory obligation.

The duty to supervise is not satisfied by the supervisor merely relying on the experience of the personnel involved. The presence of "red flags" imposes on the supervisor a duty to make an affirmative inquiry or investigation. Someone in a supervisory position cannot simply ignore or disregard "red flags" or "suggestions of irregularities;" instead, the supervisor must "act decisively to detect and prevent" improper activity. In the Matter of Grady, 1999 WL 222640 (SEC Apr. 19, 1999).

If a brokerage firm's employees in supervisory positions are put on inquiry notice that an employee may be acting improperly, the supervisor must see that the matter is investigated promptly and then take steps to follow up on the investigation. If the supervisor does not initiate his or her own investigation, he or she must direct someone else to investigate. It, thus, is not sufficient to rely simply on the employee's representations that no misconduct took place. The investigation should determine whether the conduct in fact occurred and whether there have been similar occurrences.

In the event that multiple supervisors may be involved, it is important to promptly and clearly define the responsibility of each of the supervisors in responding to the suspected wrongdoing. Again, it will be necessary to follow up in order to assure that appropriate investigatory and preventive measures have been taken. Additionally, simply reporting the suspected misconduct to a higher supervisor will not be sufficient unless the supervisor's superiors instruct him or her not to take any action. The Commission explained that appropriate supervisory action should be taken even after the matter is reported.

Instituting the investigation does not end the supervisor's responsibilities. Prompt action should be taken to prevent repetition of the suspected misconduct. This would include increased supervision of the suspected employee. It, thus, is not sufficient simply to tell the employee that the matter is under investigation and that his or her career may be in jeopardy.

b. *Rogue Brokers*

Brokers are prohibited from engaging in transactions without giving notice to the firm. Violation of this requirement is known as "selling away." Although the practice of "selling away" violates FIN-

RA rules, it is not a *per se* violation of the SEC supervisory obligations imposed by 1934 Act § 15(b). However, a firm's supervisory obligations include the obligation to institute controls to prevent "selling away" activities.

Sometimes brokerage firms seek to avoid accountability for a failure to supervise on the grounds that the registered representative acted on his or her own and was not acting on behalf of the firm. This is often referred to as a "rogue broker" defense. The rogue broker defense will not work when the firm, through its supervisory personnel, ignored red flags concerning the activity in question or if the firm fails to institute adequate internal controls reasonably designed to prevent illegal rogue broker activities.

§ 28. Protection of Customers' Privacy

The privacy protection provisions of the Gramm–Leach–Bliley Act (GLBA) were created to increase competition among banks and other financial institutions. The sharing of consumer information impacts not only the competition among firms but also customers' privacy interests. The GLBA mandates rules prohibiting the sharing of certain customer information in order to help increase competition in financial services and also to increase consumer welfare. See, e.g. SEC Reg. S–P.

The privacy regulations accomplish three basic goals. First, financial institutions, including broker-dealers, must provide a "clear and conspicuous" notice to covered customers setting forth the firm's privacy policies. The required notice must describe the conditions under which the nonpublic information about its customers may be shared with both affiliates of the firm and non-affiliated third parties. Second, the firm must provide covered customers with an opportunity to opt out of the firm's sharing of nonpublic personal information with third parties. Third, firms are required to establish policies and procedures that are reasonably designed to protect customer privacy by protecting customer records from anticipated threats, hazards, unauthorized access, or unauthorized use that could cause "substantial harm or inconvenience" to the customer.

SEC Reg. S–P establishes privacy rules that apply to brokers, dealers, and investment companies whether or not they are registered with the SEC, as well as registered investment advisers. The rules also apply to foreign (non-resident) brokers, dealers, investment companies, and investment advisers registered with the SEC, but not to those firms that are not registered with the SEC. Reg. S–P serves three functions in its application to covered broker-dealers. First, a broker-dealer must "provide notice to customers about its privacy policies and practices." Second, the rules describe "the conditions under which a financial institution may disclose nonpublic personal information about consumers to nonaffiliated third parties." Third, Regulation S–P "provides a method for consumers to prevent a financial institution from disclosing nonpublic personal information to most nonaffiliated third parties by 'opting out' of that disclosure."

SEC Reg. S–P does not preempt state laws that provide greater protection for consumers.

§ 29. State Registration Requirements for Broker–Dealers and Registered Representatives

Federal regulation of broker-dealers and associated persons is supplemented in many states by state registration requirements. State registration requirements can cover not only broker-dealer firms but also can extend to registration of registered representatives. The states have the right to require registration of broker-dealers doing business in the state even though noncompliance with the registration requirements may have the effect of precluding broker-dealers from dealing with customers in other states as well. Thus, for example, use of unregistered representatives for cold calling operations will support revocation of state broker-dealer registration. A broker-dealer's violations in connection with public offerings have also been the basis for revocation of a state broker-dealer registration. Thus, there is a variety of improper conduct that can lead to revocation of a broker-dealer's registration under state law. Violation of a state's broker-dealer registration requirements can result in civil liability to customers that engaged in securities transactions through the unregistered broker-dealer. Failure to register can also result in a criminal conviction.

The state registration requirements for broker-dealers parallel the SEC and FINRA registration requirements. As is the case with the SEC, state regulators have the power to order administrative sanctions, including restitution to injured customers.

§ 30. Municipal Securities Dealers

a. *The Municipal Securities Markets*

Municipal securities, as referred to in the 1934 Act, comprise a wide variety of obligations, primarily bonds issued by state, local or other political subdivisions or their agencies, as well as industrial development bonds. Because of their governmental issue or guarantee, municipal securities are generally exempt from the registration and reporting provisions of both the 1933 and 1934 Acts.

Transactions in municipal securities generally take place in more specialized markets by brokers and dealers dealing exclusively with municipal securities and who are, therefore, exempt from the general broker-dealer regulation and rules of the SEC. There is no organized exchange subject to SEC oversight nor is there NASD nor FINRA coverage regarding persons dealing only in municipal securities. Furthermore, prior to 1975, the Securities and Exchange Commission had no jurisdiction over these transactions except in circumstances involving fraud. The antifraud provisions that are applicable to municipal securities provide some protection to investors but significantly less than investors in securities of private issuers. Even with the municipal securities regulation that was added to the 1934 Act in 1975, the 1933 Securities Act's exemptions and the lack of an organized exchange leave investors with less protection than with the regular securities market for private issuers. Notwithstanding the 1933 Act exemption from registration, when municipal securities are initially offered to the general public by virtue of 1934 Act Rule 15c2–12, municipal securities dealers must provide a disclosure document that somewhat parallel those that would be required in a 1933 Act registration.

The early 1970s witnessed a lack of investor confidence in the municipal securities markets. At the same time, the SEC instituted several fraud actions involving municipal securities dealers that were unregulated but nevertheless subject to the Exchange Act's antifraud proscriptions. These and other factors led Congress to conclude in 1975 that "[e]xpanding the protections generally available under the federal securities laws to investors in municipal securities is * * * appropriate." Sen. Rep. No. 94–75 p. 3 (Banking, Housing and Urban Affairs Committee April 25, 1975). This led to the adoption of 1934 Act § 15B's regulation of municipal securities dealers.

b. *The Municipal Securities Industry*

There are three principal participants in the municipal securities industry. Securities firms, or "dealers," trade in municipal securities for their own account. "Dealer-banks," as is the case with securities firms acting as "dealers," trade for their own account. Thirdly, bond brokers act as agents for buyers and sellers of municipal securities. The underwriting and syndication of municipal securities are governed by state law. General obligation bonds are generally issued only after competitive bidding, while revenue bonds are typically sold on the basis of terms negotiated by the issuing governmental entity.

c. *Overview of Municipal Securities Dealer Regulation*

Since 1975, brokers and dealers, including most banks or "separately identifiable departments" thereof, not already registered under 1934 Act § 15 must register pursuant to 1934 Act § 15B(a)(1) if they use the United States mails, telephones, or other instrumentality of interstate commerce to trade municipal securities, even if they transact only intrastate business. Issuers and the securities themselves, however, are still exempt from 1934 Act registration.

Regulation of municipal securities dealers is not carried out by the SEC even though the SEC retains enforcement powers. The registration provisions are administered by the Municipal Securities Rulemaking Board (MSRB) to disclose "information generally available from other sources" than the issuer itself. 1934 Act § 15B(d)(2). Generally, this requirement simply means the broker or dealer must believe that the securities are "bona fide." MSRB Rule G–14. Municipal securities dealers are also under an obligation to make a reasonable effort to obtain a fair price for the customer. When executing a transaction in municipal securities for or on behalf of a customer as agent, a municipal securities dealer must do so at a price that is fair and reasonable in relation to prevailing market conditions. MSRB Rule G–18. This is comparable to the best execution obligation for regular securities broker-dealers.

d. *The MSRB*

The primary difference between the SROs and the MSRB is that some covered brokers are members of the SROs. The MSRB is a regulatory, nonmembership organization with primary rulemaking authority over municipal securities brokers and dealers. The Board consists of fifteen members. The membership of the MSRB "shall at all times be equally divided among public representatives, broker-dealer representatives, and bank representatives." 1934 Act § 15B(b)(2)(B). The board members are elected in accordance with procedures established in the MSRB rules. The selection of public representatives is subject to SEC approval in order to assure their independence from the broker-dealer and banking industries. As is the case with the self-regulatory organizations under the Exchange Act, the SEC has oversight responsibilities with respect to the MSRB. The SEC has statutory power to force the MSRB to adopt, abrogate, or modify any MSRB rules and to sanction or remove board members.

The MSRB has authority to set requirements for examination and qualification for municipal securities brokers and dealers, with such examinations being administered by the appropriate regulatory agency for its non-broker-dealer members such as banks, and by the SEC for other brokers and dealers. Though the MSRB has authority to set record-keeping requirements for municipal securities brokers and dealers, compliance with SEC Rules 17a–3 and 17a–4 is a satisfactory substitute.

The MSRB also has jurisdiction over disputes between municipal securities dealers. In carrying out this authority the MSRB can refer such inter-dealer disputes to binding arbitration.

e.   Enforcement

The MSRB has no enforcement power, but must instead seek the aid of the SEC, FINRA, or "appropriate regulatory agency" to apply sanctions against municipal securities brokers and dealers. These sanctions can include any that may be ordinarily imposed against other brokers and dealers. 1934 Act § 15B(c)(7) requires that before such investigation or proceeding is taken against a particular broker or dealer, the SEC and the appropriate regulatory agency must consult and cooperate with each other; however, neither the SEC nor the agency is bound by the other's decision or recommendations. If a broker or dealer is sanctioned or expelled for a municipal securities violation, the sanction applies during the period of suspension to any securities dealings he or she might undertake.

§ 31. Regulation of Government Securities Dealers

As mentioned earlier, brokers and dealers who deal solely in exempted securities need not register under 1934 Act § 15. Municipal securities dealers, who are also exempt from broker-dealer registration, are regulated through the MSRB, but there was no comparable regulation for government securities dealers until 1986. Following the insolvency of a number of government securities dealers, Congress enacted legislation to require the regulation of government securities dealers. Generally, the government securities dealer registration requirements more closely parallel that of broker-dealers than of municipal securities dealers.

a. *Definition of Government Securities*

Government securities are those securities which are issued or guaranteed by the federal government or a federal agency. Treasury securities, such as savings bonds, "T–Bills," and "Treasury Notes" are familiar government securities. Lesser-known government-guaranteed securities are those issued by federally-owned agencies, for example, Government National Mortgage Obligations or "GinnieMaes." Finally, there are money market instruments such as "federal funds" and "repurchase agreements." Federal funds are cash reserves that the Federal Reserve Board requires banks to maintain for liquidity purposes and that are manipulated by the Federal Reserve Board to effectuate monetary policy. "Repurchase agreements," or "repos," are investment schemes by which institutional investors and government securities dealers exchange cash for government securities.

b. *Scope of Government Securities Dealer Regulation*

The market for United States government securities has been described as the world's largest, most efficient and liquid securities market. Senate Report No. 99–426, S. 1416, Government Securities Act of 1986 at 5 (Sept. 17, 1986). The United States Treasury uses the market to finance the national debt, while the Federal Reserve Board conducts monetary policy through the market. As such, the government securities market is "the cornerstone of the U.S. capital market system," and its integrity must be insured. However, between July 1975 and April 1985, failures of unregistered government securities dealers threatened this integrity. Certain problems were common to many of the failures. In some cases the failed firm had issued false and misleading financial statements; or in some cases a firm would mask its troubled status through complex relationships and transactions with affiliated companies; and finally, customer losses often occurred because the customer failed to secure control of or collateralize securities underlying a repurchase (or "repo") transaction with a problem dealer. Congress identified the weakness of the regulatory framework for the government securities market as a major cause of these failures. To bolster this framework, Congress enacted the Government Securities Act of 1986.

The Government Securities Act of 1986 added 1934 Act § 15C. The Government Securities Act of 1986 seeks to eliminate those problems identified by Congress by: (1) requiring registration of government securities brokers and dealers with the Commission or with appropriate regulatory agencies; (2) establishing financial responsibility safeguards such as capital adequacy and reporting requirements; (3) mandating procedures for the acceptance and use of customers' securities; and (4) allowing on-site inspection and enforcement by federal regulators. The Government Securities Act of 1986 was also designed not to impose regulation that will adversely affect the liquidity and efficiency of the government securities market.

c. *Types of Government Securities Dealers*

There are three varieties of dealers who participate in the government securities markets: primary dealers, inter-dealer brokers, and secondary dealers. The Federal Reserve Bank of New York carries out the Federal Reserve Board's monetary policy through primary dealers. In addition to acting as the exclusive traders with the Federal Reserve Bank of New York, primary dealers also engage in trading among themselves and between secondary dealers. The primary dealers engage in these transactions through inter-dealer brokers. These inter-dealer transactions are conducted through electronic quotations that do not display parties to the transaction and thus are known as "blind brokering." Primary dealers and inter-dealer brokers make up the lion's share of the government securities market in terms of trading volume.

d. *Registration of Government Securities Dealers; Definitions, Exemptions and Exclusions*

The Government Securities Act of 1986 requires brokers and dealers engaged exclusively in the business of buying and selling government securities to register with the SEC. Whether or not an entity falls within the definition of government security dealer is decided in much the same way as securities broker-dealers generally.

Brokers and dealers already registered with the Commission because of their general securities business, and financial institutions already subject to the regulatory jurisdiction of another federal government agency, as well as primary dealers, are not required to register. However, SEC registered brokers and dealers, financial institutions, and primary dealers are required to notify the appropriate regulatory agency of their status as a government securities broker or dealer.

In addition to having to register with the SEC, all government securities brokers and dealers that are required to register with the SEC are also required to become members of an SRO, which in most cases would be FINRA. 1934 Act § 15C(e)(1), (2). For government securities brokers or dealers who fail to submit to these registration and membership requirements, the SEC is authorized to censure, limit, or suspend their operations. The SEC can also revoke the registration of a government securities broker or dealer who falls out of compliance with the Government Securities Act of 1986. The SEC cannot investigate violations of this section, require filings, or take any actions against government securities brokers or dealers if the SEC is not the appropriate regulatory agency for the broker or dealer. However, the appropriate regulatory agencies are vested with the same power to sanction their subject brokers or dealers as is the SEC. Finally, any registered government securities broker or dealer who wishes to withdraw from registration must do so in writing, or if the SEC determines that the business is no longer in existence, the Commission may cancel the registration.

CHAPTER 3

EXCHANGE TRADING AND MARKET MAKING

§ 32. Exchange Trading

The principal function and purpose of a national securities exchange is to provide a marketplace in which member firms, acting as brokers, can purchase and sell securities for the account of their customers. The question addressed in 1934 Act § 11 is the extent to which stock exchange members and their firms should be permitted to trade in listed securities for their own account, in view of the possibly unfair advantages they may have over public customers when engaged in such trading.

1934 Act § 11(a), as amended in 1975, prohibits an exchange member from effecting any transactions on the exchange for its own account, or any account with respect to which it exercises investment discretion, with certain specified exceptions, including transactions as a market maker (specialist) or odd-lot dealer, stabilizing transactions in connection with distributions, bona fide arbitrage transactions, and other transactions that the SEC concludes should be exempt from the prohibition. Traditionally exchange transactions were viewed as fitting into three categories: (a) "floor trading" and "off-floor trading" by members and their firms, (b) transactions by "odd-lot dealers" (firms that specialize in trades in lots other than multiples of 100 shares), and (c) transactions by specialists. More recently, the increasing domination of New York Stock Exchange trading by institutional customers has focused attention on two additional categories: (d) "block positioning" by member firms and (e) transactions for "managed institutional accounts."

Trading on traditional stock exchanges was based on a physical floor and centered around the specialist system which was designed to provide a true auction market. However, technology has made the traditional system obsolete. The advent of electronic quotations and electronic communications networks (ECNs) has moved many transactions from the exchange floor that used to be the center of trading. In fact, some exchanges, such as the NASDAQ Stock Market, are entirely virtual exchanges and do not have a physical trading floor.

§ 33. "Floor Trading;" "Off–Floor Trading;" and an Introduction to Trading Practices

The principal purpose of 1934 Act § 11(a), as originally enacted, was to authorize the SEC to write rules (1) "to regulate or prevent floor trading" by exchange members, and (2) to prevent excessive off-floor trading by members if the Commission found it "detrimental to the maintenance of a fair and orderly market."

"Floor trading" was the specialty of a small percentage of NYSE members who maintained their memberships for the sole or primary purpose of roaming around the exchange floor and trading for their own account in whatever securities caught their fancy. The SEC adopted some mild restrictions on floor trading in 1945, but nothing significant was done until 1963, when the SEC's Special Study of the Securities Markets concluded that floor trading was a vestige of the pre–1934 "private club" atmosphere of the exchanges and should be abolished. In 1964, the SEC adopted 1934 Act Rule 11a–1, prohibiting all floor trading by members, unless conducted in accordance with a plan adopted by an exchange and approved by the Commission. The NYSE simultaneously adopted a plan, which was then approved by the SEC, requiring floor traders to register with the exchange, to maintain minimum capital and pass a qualifying examination, and to comply with special restrictions on their trading activity.

In 1978, the NYSE established a new category of "registered competitive market makers" with certain responsibilities to assist the specialist (see § 35 infra) in maintaining an orderly market. As floor traders have switched over to this new category, traditional floor trading has continued to diminish in importance, amounting to only 0.02% of NYSE trading in 1989. Once the bulwark of exchange trading, floor trading may be viewed by some as nothing more than an anachronism.

As noted above, the trading floor is no longer the center of the stock exchanges. "Off-floor" trading by member firms (i.e. transactions initiated by decisions at the firm's offices, rather than on the floor), accounts for a much greater proportion of activity than floor trading, having amounted to roughly 14% of total NYSE volume in 1989. In 1999, off-floor trading amounted to 11.1% of the NYSE's total volume. This type of activity was not thought to give rise to the same kind of problems as floor trading, and for a long time the SEC did not undertake to impose any direct restrictions on it. However, after an SEC study of off-floor trading, the NYSE adopted rules designed to prevent member firms from transmitting orders to the floor ahead of their customers at times when they might be privy to "inside information."

Trading practices generally are scrutinized in an attempt to prevent manipulative practices. For example, traders, specialists, and designated market makers are subject to a best execution obligation and are also prohibited from trading ahead of their customer orders. Another prohibited practice, known as "flipping" or "trading for eighths," occurs when a broker simultaneously trades for a customer's account at a fractionally different price in order to take advantage of the spread between the bid and the asked price. Typically the broker will also charge a commission on these transactions. Violation of trading practices can result in disciplinary action including expulsion.

§ 34. Block Positioning and Institutional Membership

Institutional investors (principally pension funds, mutual funds, and insurance companies) have increased their investments in common stocks to the point that they currently account for sixty to seventy percent of the trading on the NYSE. Institutions often trade in large blocks (10,000 shares or more), which in 1999 accounted for slightly more than half of total NYSE trading volume. These block transactions put special strains on exchange market making mechanisms. If a member firm specializing in institutional business has a customer that wishes to sell 100,000 shares of a particular stock, but can only find buyers for 80,000, the firm itself will "position" the remaining 20,000 shares and then sell them off over a period of time as the market can absorb them. Thus, the member firm inherits the risk of loss due to a decline in the price of the remaining securities, and the potential to profit from an increase in the price of the remaining securities. 1934 Act § 11(a)(1)(A) recognizes this "market-making" function as a legitimate exception to the prohibition against trading by members for their own account.

Another question raised by the growth of institutional trading was whether an institutional investor (or an affiliated broker) should be permitted to become a member of an exchange and thus avoid intermediary costs in effecting transactions for the institutional investor's account. The NYSE had consistently barred institutions and their affiliates from membership. However, a number of institutions in the pre–1975 period, when fixed minimum commissions were charged on all stock exchange transactions, a number of institutional investors joined "regional" exchanges (which serve as alternative markets for most NYSE-listed stocks) to achieve greater flexibility in the use of their commission dollars or to recover a portion of the commissions for the benefit of the institutions.

The brokerage firms, alarmed at the potential loss of their biggest customers, persuaded Congress in the 1975 amendments to prevent "institutional membership" by prohibiting any exchange member from effecting any transaction on the exchange for any institutional account over which it or an affiliate exercises investment discretion. the 1975 amendments also eliminated fixed commission rates, which eliminated virtually all incentive for institutions to join exchanges, because these large institutions were then free to negotiate a discounted commission structure with exchange members. Thus, brokerage firms discovered that they (or those of them that managed institutional accounts) were the principal victims of the new prohibition, which became effective in February 1979.

§ 35. Specialists and Designated Market Makers

a. *Specialists*

Under the traditional NYSE system a specialist was a floor trader who did not have a retail securities business but as discussed below this restriction has been relaxed. Instead of handling retail customers specialists (and now designated market makers) purchase and sell securities for his or her own account or executes orders for other brokers, thus specializing in the securities of particular companies or issues. Unlike the case with the over-the-counter markets, traditional exchange traded securities did not require a market-maker to provide a central clearing house for all bid and asked quotations. However, the securities industry recognized that even within the context of a traditional physical exchange, it is necessary to maintain an "orderly market," which is free in the short run from erratic and unreasonable fluctuations in prices of particular securities to the extent possible, and to help match the bid and asked prices, between which there is usually a spread. 1934 Act § 11(b) empowers the exchanges to register specialists provided that their rules require compliance with certain conditions established by the SEC. The applicable SEC standards are set forth in 1934 Act Rule 11b–1, which requires, *inter alia,* that the exchange set minimum net capital requirements for specialists and designated market makers. The rule also requires the exchange to condition specialist status upon "the maintenance, so far as practicable, of a fair and orderly market." A specialist's continued failure to satisfy the exchange standards subjects him or her to suspension or cancellation of his registration with the exchange. Additionally, 1934 Act Rule 11b–1(a)(2)(v) requires the exchange to provide for "effective and systematic surveillance" of specialists.

SEC regulation of exchange trading is not limited to specialists and designated market makers. For example, in addition to the regulation of specialists, the 1934 Act regulates floor traders on the exchanges.

Although the specialist system has been replaced by one based on designated market makers, it is important to understand the development of these systems. Following the direction of the SEC, the New York Stock Exchange and other exchanges developed a system of specialists for each security traded, with rules enforceable by the exchange itself. The specialist firm occupies a unique dual role in the operation of the NYSE, as they do with the other securities exchanges. First, a specialist firm acts as a "broker's broker," maintaining a "book" on which other brokers can leave customers' "limit orders" (i.e., orders to buy or sell at a price at which they cannot currently be executed). Second, a specialist acts as the exclusive franchised dealer, or "market-maker" in its assigned stocks, buying and selling shares from other brokers when there are no customer orders on its book against which the orders can be matched.

The functions of the specialist can be illustrated by the following example. A firm is the specialist in an actively traded stock, in which the market is $40 to $40.10. This means that customer orders are on the specialist's book to buy specified numbers of shares at $40 or less, and other orders are on his book to sell at $40.10 or more (for historical reasons, shares formerly were quoted in halves, quarters, and eighths rather than cents but now are traded in decimals). A broker who comes to the specialist with an order to sell "at the market" will sell to the customer with the first buy order on the book at $40, and a broker who comes with a market order to buy at the market will buy from the customer with the first sell order on the book at $40.10. The specialist acts solely as a subagent, receiving a portion of the "book" customer's commission to his broker.

Now assume the same firm is also a specialist in an inactively traded stock. The only orders on the book are an order to buy at $38 and an order to sell at $42. If the specialist acted solely as agent, a broker who came in with a market order to sell would receive $38, and another broker who came in an hour later with a market order to buy would pay $42. The report of these two trades on the "tape" would indicate the stock had risen 4 points, or more than 10%, in an hour. The exchange therefore imposes an obligation on the specialist to maintain an "orderly market" in his or her assigned stocks, buying and selling for his own account to even out swings which would result from buyers and sellers not appearing at his post at the same time. In this case he might make his market at $40 to $40.25, trading for his own account as long as necessary, but yielding priority to customers' orders on his book whenever they provide as good a price to the party on the other side.

While this combination of functions has obvious advantages, it also offers possibilities for abuse. With his monopoly trading position and knowledge of the "book," the specialist, by moving the price of his specialty stocks up and down, can guarantee himself profits in both his "broker" and "dealer" functions. The SEC has from time to time studied and expressed its concern about this problem but has never undertaken direct regulation of specialists' activities. In 1965, it adopted 1934 Act Rule 11b–1, requiring the principal exchanges to maintain and enforce rules designed to curb abuses by specialists, but recent SEC and Congressional studies have expressed continuing dissatisfaction with NYSE surveillance and regulation of specialist activities. In recent years, however, the NYSE has disciplined a number of specialists for improper trades or reports of trades, failure to maintain orderly markets, and other violations.

In 1975, Congress amended 1934 Act § 11(b) to make clear that the SEC had authority to limit specialists to acting either as brokers or dealers, but not both, but the SEC has not yet taken any action pursuant to this authority. For a long time, the exchanges took the view that by barring retail brokers from the specialist function, they were preventing possible conflicts of interest. However, pressure from the brokerage industry and the exchanges' desire to remain competitive with the over-the-counter markets where there are no such limitations on market-makers has made inroads on the long-time separation of functions. The ground rules are changing. The Pacific and Boston stock exchanges allowed diversified firms (i.e. those engaging in retail or other brokerage activities) to act as specialists. The American Exchange's Board of Governors has approved a similar measure, and the NYSE has also adopted a proposal that would allow diversified firms to act as specialists. Retail brokers are now permitted to acquire specialist firms and avoid certain specialist restrictions by imposing information barriers (a Chinese Wall or fire wall). See § 42 infra. Those avoided restrictions include: (1) trading specialty securities, (2) trading options on specialty securities (other than for hedging purposes), (3) accepting orders for specialty securities from institutions, the issuer and its insiders, (4) performing research and advisory services with respect to specialty securities, and (5) transacting business with a company in whose stock the specialist is registered.

To the extent that the specialist does not operate at the retail level, there is no possibility of a conflict of interest such as that which can arise with a market-maker in the over-the-counter markets. However, a higher standard of conduct is imposed on the specialist than the mere avoidance of fraud; he or she must act so as not to cause investors to be concerned about his honesty. Furthermore, the specialist is subject to very strict surveillance. Approximately eight times each year there are random, detailed one-week inspections of each specialist's activities by the exchange. This is in addition to requiring each specialist to make his books available to the exchange inspection, which will reveal the details of each transaction. Specialists are subject to special capital requirements imposed by their respective exchanges and are limited in their dealings with the issuers of the particular stocks, large institutional investors, other broker-dealers (for public customers), and in the purchase and sale of large blocks either individually or as members of a pool.

b. Designated Market Makers and the Demise of the Specialist

In 2008, the NYSE replaced the conventional "specialist" system with a new system centered on the "designated market maker" or "DMM." Sec. Exch. Act Rel. No. 34–58845 (SEC Oct. 29, 2008). This official name change reflects important policy modifications implemented by the NYSE regarding the role of the firms that were typically referred to as specialists. The new system was set up to be implemented in phases. When fully implemented, the designated market maker system will result in a number of significant changes to the ways in which these firms operated under the specialist system. Three systemic changes were identified in the applicable SEC release: "(i) The phasing out of the specialist system and adopting a Designated Market Maker ('DMM') structure; (ii) the alteration of NYSE's priority and parity rules, most significantly to allow DMMs to trade on parity with orders on

NYSE's Display Book("Display Book"); and (iii) the introduction of new order functionality, including the DMM Capital Commitment Schedule ("CCS") and hidden orders."

In order to achieve parity between DMMs and other market makers, unlike specialists, DMMs will no longer have access to exclusive advanced looks at incoming trade orders. Instead, the DMMs receive the same information, at the same time, that is made available to other market participants. Due to this new parity, DMMs are no longer subject to the specialist's "negative obligation" regarding trading in their own accounts and now are allowed to trade for their own account. This change was implemented to provide more equality among all trading parties and thus to help accomplish better pricing and more efficiency overall in the trading process.

As a result of the phasing out of the specialist system, the NYSE now allows for more integration between the upstairs and downstairs operations of trading firms. Previously, the specialist operation was required to be a separate unit of the firm; the new DMM units may now interact with the retail (or upstairs) operations provided certain specific procedures are followed. This integration of operations should allow DMMs access to more capital and create more cost-effective operations and overall efficiencies, resulting in a deeper and broader market. Along with these recent major policy shifts, the NYSE rules still impose an affirmative obligation on DMMs to commit their own capital when necessary to combat pricing problems due to imbalances or illiquidity. The overall result of these comprehensive NYSE policies is designed to improve the speed, liquidity, and fairness of trading for all market participants.

§ 36. Technological   Advancements–Impact on Exchange Trading

Technological advancements led to questions concerning the continued viability of the specialist system and, as described in the preceding section, to the eventual replacement of specialists with designated market makers. Under a system of screen-based trading, market professionals can execute transactions without the aid of an intermediary such as a specialist or a market-maker. Screen-based trading differs from an automated quotation system such as NASDAQ in that the quotation system merely delivers the current quotes, while a screen-based trading system permits actual "real time" execution of orders. In its adoption of a limited after hours trading program, the NYSE ventured into screen-based trading, initially on a limited basis. Some foreign exchanges have made the shift to screen-based trading and away from floor trading on an across-the-board basis. This is the also the case with the NASDAQ Stock Market that does not have a physical trading floor.

The International Organization of Securities Commissions adopted a set of general principles governing the operation of screen-based systems. The ten principles, which are intended to serve as a guide for developers of screen-based systems and regulators, address financial integrity, surveillance, and disclosure, as well as operational issues including access to the system, system vulnerability, and security.

First, the sponsor of the screen-based trading system should be able to demonstrate to the applicable regulatory agency that the system meets applicable legal standards, regulatory policies, and/or relevant market customs and practices. Second, the system should "ensure the equitable availability of accurate and timely trade and quotation information" to all participants in the system. The processing, prioritization, and display of quotations within the system should be described to the applicable regulatory agency. Third, the sponsor of the screen-based trading system should describe to the relevant regulatory authorities the order execution algorithm, which is the system's rule structure for processing, prioritizing, and executing orders. Fourth, the system should be technically designed so as to operate "in a manner equitable to all market participants" and the system sponsor should describe any differences in treatment between categories of participants. Fifth, prior to implementation and periodically thereafter, the system should undergo an objective risk assessment as to the system's vulnerability to unauthorized access, internal failures, human errors, attacks, and natural catastrophes. Sixth, the system should develop procedures to monitor the competence, integrity, and authority of system users; system users should be supervised and should not arbitrarily or discriminatorily be denied access to the system. Seventh, the system sponsor and appropriate regulatory authorities should consider risk management exposures, including those stemming from interfacing with related financial systems. Eighth, there should be mechanisms in place for adequate surveillance of the system for both supervisory and enforcement purposes. The surveillance mechanisms should be available to the appropriate regulatory authorities as well as to the system sponsor. Ninth, the system sponsor and appropriate regulatory authorities should see to it that there is adequate risk disclosure to system users resulting from use of the system. In addition to disclosure of the significant risks of system use, there should be a description of the system sponsor's and providers' liability to system subscribers and users. Tenth, there should be procedures to ensure that the system sponsor, system providers, and system users be made aware of and be responsive to the directives and concerns of the appropriate regulatory authorities.

Enhanced technology and screen-based trading has not been without its problems. For example, as mentioned earlier (see § 9 supra), in May 2010, the markets experienced a "flash crash" causing the market to tumble precipitously and then recover most of its losses within matters of hours. The SEC and the various markets instituted a study and imposed a pilot program of circuit breakers designed to prevent a reoccurrence of such extreme intra-day volatility.

Online trading has opened up new horizons for trading opportunities. An Internet service that matches customer orders for securities may have to register under the 1934 Act as an exchange. See BondGlobe, 2001 WL 103418 (SEC No Action Letter Feb. 6, 2001). The SEC, in Reg. ATS, has adopted standards for acceptable alternative trading systems.

In 1996, there was some controversy over the emergence of the use of the Internet for securities trading. For example, the SEC was concerned about a small brewery that used the Internet to accomplish an initial public offering and then make a market in its shares. The SEC seriously questioned this offering and these activities were subsequently halted, but after negotiations, the SEC permitted trading to resume with certain safeguards. Additionally, the SEC subsequently issued a no action letter permitting a company to make a market in its own shares using the Internet. Real Goods Trading Corp., 1996 WL 422670 (SEC No Action Letter June 25, 1996). Beyond Internet offerings, considerable problems can occur when a market-maker is also acting as an underwriter for the company in a public offering. Although this is a perfectly permissible dual role, it does present all sorts of opportunities for illegal manipulation. (See § 41 infra).

§ 37. NASDAQ and OTC Market–Making

Since the OTC markets by definition do not have a central exchange for the entering of buy and sell orders, it is necessary to have some sort of central clearing house to perform a comparable function. NASDAQ is merely an electronic means of publicizing the latest quotes but is not a vehicle for effecting transactions. NASDAQ generally gives both "bid" and "asked" quotes for over-the-counter securities. Several hundred of the more actively traded over-the-counter securities are listed on a "national market" with only one quoted price.

Traditionally, quotations for securities not traded through the national market system or automated quotation system were found in the "pink sheets." The SEC approved, originally on a one-year pilot basis, a NASD electronic bulletin board for computerized quotations for stocks not listed on a national exchange or in the NASDAQ system. As anticipated, to a large extent these electronic bulletin boards have replaced the pink sheets. Also, in conjunction with its adoption of 1933 Act Rule 144A, the SEC approved the NASD's screen-based computer and communication system called PORTAL (Private Offerings, Resales and Trading through Automated Linkages) to facilitate secondary trading of Rule 144A securities. PORTAL has become a significant avenue for secondary trading in unregistered securities of both domestic and foreign issuers. As already noted, in 2006, the NASDAQ Stock Market registered with the SEC as a national securities exchange and thus no longer qualifies as an over-the-counter market. Smaller cap stocks traded through NASDAQ but not on the NASDAQ Stock Market remain over-the-counter.

Most NASDAQ and OTC trades take place through online communications among securities dealers and using quotations provided by market-makers. The enhanced technology presents the opportunity for magnifying the effects of human error by transferring that misinformation more rapidly and efficiently into the marketplace.

§ 38.   Market–Makers and the Obligation to Maintain an Orderly Market

The national securities exchanges, modeled on an auction paradigm, operate in such a way as to match customers seeking to sell securities with those seeking to buy. See § 6 supra. The OTC and NASDAQ markets do not operate as a traditional exchange as they are not centrally organized. In order to maintain a market for securities without a central exchange, designated broker-dealers operate as "market-makers" in the over-the-counter and NASDAQ markets, buying and selling as principals for their own account rather than as agents for customers.

The concept of market-maker is defined broadly to include dealers who hold themselves out as willing to purchase and sell a particular security for their own account "on a regular or continuous basis." 1934 Act § 3(a)(38). It is not necessary that the dealer hold itself out in any particular manner, thus raising the possibility of inadvertent market-maker status. Attainment of market-maker status will exempt the dealer from some provisions of the securities laws that otherwise would apply, such as

1934 Act § 16(b)'s prohibitions against short-swing profits. Additionally, market-making activities are closely scrutinized by the SEC and FINRA (and formerly by the NASD).

§ 39. FINRA and NASD Regulation of Market–Makers

The FINRA (formerly NASD) Conduct Rules establish standards of conduct for market-makers to assure that they carry out their operations in an appropriate manner. Thus, for example, a broker-dealer who accepts payment for its decision to act as a market-maker has compromised its position of neutrality and therefore will be subject to SEC sanctions. The acceptance of compensation interferes with the normal factors a broker-dealer should consider in deciding whether to act as market-maker; such factors include those that affect the security's liquidity and intrinsic value. The market-maker's obligation is to maintain an orderly market. However, when the market-maker is executing customer orders, its primary obligation is to those customers. Eichler v. SEC, 757 F.2d 1066 (9th Cir. 1985)

A broker-dealer acts as a market-maker for a particular security or securities. Many securities have more than one market-maker. A market-maker for a particular security not traded on a national exchange must enter "bid" and "asked" quotes either in the "pink sheets" or over NASDAQ. The NASD rules provide that a market maker can qualify as a Primary NASDAQ Market–Maker ("PNMM"). In part because of the potential for

abuse resulting from control of the market, NAS-
DAQ stocks must be handled by at least three
market makers. The presence of multiple market
makers does not eliminate the potential for collusion. It is possible that two of the market makers
are truly passive, resulting in one dominating market maker. In addition, a dealer with only a small
percentage of the total market float (i.e. the shares
held by the public) could potentially participate in
manipulative market making practices. FINRA's
market-maker regulations are supplemented by the
Exchange Act's antifraud provisions.

A market-maker's obligations include the posting
of reliable quotations that are not the result of
market manipulation. The market-maker is also
obligated to honor the quotations that it posts to
the market. Accordingly, it violates FINRA (and
formerly NASD) rules if a market-maker fails to
honor posted quotes. A market-maker is responsible
for making "two-way" bids on the securities for
which it makes a market. In other words, the market-maker has the responsibility of quoting both a
bid price (the price that someone is willing to pay
for the security) or an offer wanted (OW), as well as
an asked price (the price at which someone is willing to sell the security) or a bid wanted (BW). As
such, the market-maker must be willing to stand
behind these quotations and advertisements for offers and bids wanted. He or she thus must be
willing and prepared to both buy the stock or sell it
as principal, depending upon the demands of the
market. Accordingly, the market-maker is frequent-

ly in the position of holding long and short positions in the securities in which he or she makes the market. The SEC rules require that the market maker is financially able to fulfill these obligations. In general, market-makers are subject to significant regulation by both the NASD and SEC, including inspection of records in order to assure that they are not abusing their market making positions. 1934 Act Rule 17a–5(a). The SEC rules also give the FINRA supervisory power, which includes the ability to withdraw a broker-dealer's market making authority.

§ 40. Market–Makers' Conflict of Interest; Disclosure Obligations

In an attempt to promote the more efficient execution of customer orders and more accurate pricing, as well as to eliminate potential conflicts of interest, the SEC approved the NASD's prohibition against market-makers trading ahead of certain customer orders. Exch. Act Rel. No. 34–34279, 59 Fed. Reg. 34,883 (SEC July 7, 1994). The NASD rules which are now part of FINRA's regulatory scheme apply to all NASDAQ-traded securities and prohibit broker-dealers acting in their market making capacity from trading ahead of their customers' limit orders.

§ 41. Market–Makers and Manipulation

Market-makers can abuse their positions by engaging in manipulative practices. The NASD watches closely to assure that the market-maker in fact maintains an orderly market and is not engaging in manipulative practices; if so, the market-maker will be subject to losing approval to act as a market-maker. The risk of market-maker manipulation is much greater when a broker-dealer acts as the sole market-maker for the stock in question. When brokerage firms enter into transactions with respect to their "house stocks," there is no independent free market to gauge the legitimacy of the firm's market making and other activities in connection with those transactions. Brokerage houses handling house stocks are thus in a very good position to manipulate the market. Thus, although there is nothing illegal *per se* about concentrating in house stocks, doing so is one of the common indicators of a controlled market manipulation. Other manipulative activities can also occur in connection with house stocks. For example, account representatives may be given higher commissions for pushing "house stocks." They may also be given disincentives for having customers enter sell orders in house stocks. In extreme instances, customer sell orders may even be ignored. These practices, which are designed to dissuade customer sales orders, constitute illegal manipulation and also violate broker-dealer standards of fair dealing.

Control over the market is not in itself a violation of the 1934 Act. However, the failure to disclose control over the market for securities handled by the market-maker and broker-dealer is a violation of the antifraud provisions. Also, by controlling and cornering the market by reducing the market float and thereby decreasing supply, or by artificially reducing supply through market squeezes, broker-dealers can illegally maintain artificially high prices in the stocks they are manipulating. Market domination frequently is part of successful manipulative schemes. See §§ 50–51, 65–66 infra.

A market-maker's domination of the market can arise from natural market forces, such as the other market-makers not taking as active an interest in the stock or not being willing to offer better bid and asked prices based on their own independent judgment. Thus, the existence of dominance and control may not be *per se* manipulation. When that domination is achieved through intentional conduct by the dominant market-maker or through collusion, then there is a manipulation taking place. A dominated, and hence noncompetitive, market will enable the dominant market-maker to maintain larger spreads and thereby reap greater market making profits. The existence of larger spreads may be the result of an inactive market, and standing alone will not establish that the market has been manipulated.

Where there are multiple market-makers, there is the potential for collusion and price fixing. Price fixing violates the antitrust laws and will result in damages to the customers who are injured as a result of the collusion in pricing. Other collusive or anticompetitive activity among market-makers may also involve violations of the SEC's manipulation prohibitions. Most conduct of broker-dealers that is regulated by the SEC and the self-regulatory organizations is not subject to antitrust scrutiny. Accordingly, at least one court has held that SEC regulation of market making activities operates as an implied repeal of the antitrust laws in connection with market making. In re Stock Exchanges Options Trading Antitrust Litigation, 2001 WL 128325 (S.D.N.Y. 2001) (when Congress empowered the SEC to regulate options trading, it impliedly repealed the antitrust laws with regard to such activity). See also, e.g, Credit Suisse Securities (USA) LLC v. Billing, 551 U.S. 264 (2007) (public offering practices were immune from antitrust attack because of their regulation under the securities laws); Friedman v. Salomon/Smith Barney, Inc., 313 F.3d 796 (2d Cir. 2002) (implied immunity barred antitrust price fixing attack on broker-dealer practices designed to restrict flipping in IPO transactions).

CHAPTER 4

RETAIL AND OTHER OPERATIONS

§ 42. Multiservice Brokerage Firms; The Chinese Wall or Fire Wall

At the time that the federal securities laws were originally enacted, the functions of the various professionals in the securities industry were relatively distinct. However, the last quarter of the twentieth century witnessed not only the elimination of clear distinctions between the permissible activities of banks and securities firms, but also the proliferation of multiservice firms providing a wide variety of financial services. Thus, for example, today, a multiservice securities firm combines the functions of investment banking and corporate counseling with investment advisory, investment management, and retail broker-dealer services.

Brokerage firms that offer a wide variety of services are required to separate the operations of many of those services. This separation is not limited to operations but also involves accounting and recordkeeping issues. Furthermore, information barriers known as "Chinese walls" or "fire walls" may have to be established in order to avoid conflict of interest problems.

on independent research, not from confidential information acquired from the firm's other departments. The anti-fraud provisions of the security laws require the firm to disclose all material nonpublic information it has or abstain from using it in trading or recommending the security in question. This "disclose or abstain" rule further obligates firms to refrain from executing or recommending transactions unless justified in light of all information known to the firm. In response to these conflicting duties, multiservice financial institutions have established internal policies and procedures to restrict the flow of material nonpublic information from the department in which it originates. These procedures are colloquially referred to as "Chinese Walls" or "fire walls."

The Chinese Wall, fire wall, or information barrier concept in securities law originated in the settlement of a Securities and Exchange Commission proceeding against Merrill Lynch in a case involving the misuse of inside information. In the Matter of Merrill Lynch, Pierce, Fenner and Smith, Inc., Sec. Exchange Act Release No. 8459, [1967–69 Transfer Binder] Fed.Sec.L.Rep. (CCH) ¶ 77,629 (1968). Merrill Lynch, while serving as the managing underwriter for an offering of Douglas Aircraft securities, passed on non-public information concerning an expected drop in earnings to favored Merrill Lynch customers who in turn sold their Douglas Aircraft holdings. After having initiated proceedings against Merrill Lynch and certain of its employees, the SEC and Merrill Lynch entered into a settlement order.

In accepting Merrill Lynch's offer of settlement, the SEC highlighted Merrill Lynch's new procedures for preventing dissemination of confidential non-public information by the underwriting department to other branches of the firm. The procedures implemented by Merrill Lynch, though not expressly named, have come to be known as Chinese Walls. While the SEC endorsed Merrill Lynch's new procedures, the SEC did not give blanket approval to the use of Chinese Walls or information barriers as a cure-all. The SEC stated, "[a]s a matter of Commission policy, we do not, and indeed cannot, determine in advance that the Statement of Policy will prove adequate in all circumstances that may arise."

Since the *Merrill Lynch* case, although the SEC continues to rely on the Chinese Wall, fire wall, or information barrier in settling administrative proceedings, the development of case law in this area has been sparse. In Slade v. Shearson, Hammill & Co., 517 F.2d 398 (2d Cir. 1974) the Second Circuit, while not taking a position on the Chinese Wall, discussed its implications. Shearson, Hammill argued that the federal securities laws precluded it from using inside information to the benefit of its customers and therefore recommended placing a Chinese Wall between its departments to prevent the passage of confidential information. The plaintiffs did not attack the concept of the Chinese Wall or information barrier but found fault with the assertion that the securities laws prevent a broker from ending a selling campaign once it has received adverse inside information concerning the issuer.

The SEC, in an attempt to reconcile the principles that inside information should not lead to market profits and that brokers should deal fairly with their customers, advocated a reinforced Chinese Wall composed of a ban on transmission of inside information between departments, strengthened by a list of companies whose securities the firm could not recommend because of an existing bank relationship.

The SEC again indicated approval of the Chinese Wall in 1934 Act Rule 14e–3, adopted in 1980 to prohibit insider trading by those in possession of material nonpublic information in connection with tender offers. Paragraph (b) of the rule provides a safe harbor exclusion for firms adopting a Chinese Wall if the firm is able to show that (1) the individual making the investment decision had no knowledge of the non-public material information and (2) the firm had implemented "one or a combination of policies and procedures, reasonable under the circumstances" to ensure that those making investment decisions for the firm do not violate Rule 14e–3. Rule 14e–3 thus is the SEC's formalization of the propriety of the Chinese Wall or information barrier as a way of avoiding liability for misuse of information.

A financial services firm carries the burden of proof to demonstrate its satisfaction of both elements of the safe harbor. The SEC specified two procedures in the rule—(1) a Chinese Wall and (2) identifying securities that are on a restricted list and thus would not be covered by research reports

or recommendations to customers. It is important
to note that the SEC, in its release adopting 1934
Act Rule 14e–3, stated that a broker-dealer may not
continue to trade for its own account when the
broker-dealer possesses material, non-public information relating to the tender offer. SEC Exchange
Act Rel. No. 34–17120 [1980 Transfer Binder] Fed.
Sec.L.Rep. (CCH) ¶ 82,646 (Sept. 4, 1980). The SEC
also stated that when a broker-dealer or other financial services institution uses a Chinese Wall, "it
may be appropriate to advise customers of its use of
such procedure * * * because [this disclosure would
alert customers that] the institution would not be
using all information it had received to the benefit
of a particular customer." Another use of the Chinese wall (or fire wall) is to permit retail brokers to
acquire exchange specialists without running afoul
of the restrictions of specialist activity.

The Chinese Wall procedures are not limited to
brokerage firms but also apply to investment companies. Thus, for example, the SEC adopted ICA
Rule 17j–1, which addresses certain insider trading-
type problems impacting upon investment companies. The rule requires registered investment companies to adopt a written code of ethics containing
provisions reasonably necessary to prevent its access persons from engaging in any activity prohibited by the securities acts' general anti-fraud provisions. This would include information barriers to
prevent the potential for insider trading. Further,
the rule requires that investment companies use
reasonable diligence and institute procedures rea-

sonably necessary to prevent violations of the code. Any director, officer, general partner, or advisory person who acquires direct or indirect beneficial ownership of any security as defined in the rule is required to report such transactions to their investment company adviser or underwriter. In the release accompanying the rule, the SEC stated that it expected that certain abusive activities would be specifically considered in the codes of ethics adopted by the registered investment companies.

Further SEC approval of the Chinese Wall concept can be found in 1933 Act Rules 137, 138, and 139. Recognizing the fact that multi-service firms have research analysts separate from the underwriting department, Rules 137, 138, and 139 permit the research department to operate without violating Section 5 of the 1933 Act as long as internal controls are implemented to insure that the two departments are separate. In 2002, the SEC announced that it was considering a proposal to require brokerage firms to spin-off their research operations. This never came to pass because of industry concerns that independent research firms would result in less information generally available to investors. There remains considerable concern about conflicts of interest that can arise with respect to brokerage firm analyst recommendations. See § 61 infra.

In 1984, the Insider Trading Sanctions Act (Pub. Law 98–376) introduced treble damages for civil liability in SEC insider trading enforcement cases. In considering the Insider Trading Sanctions Act, both Houses of Congress had occasion to consider the Chinese Wall concept. The House Committee Report in recognizing the SEC's endorsement of the Chinese Wall states, "In this context, it is also important to recognize that, under both existing law and the bill, a multiservice firm with an effective Chinese Wall would not be liable for trades effected on one side of the wall, notwithstanding inside information possessed by firm employees on the other side." House Committee Report (on ITSA) No. 98–355; 98th Congress 1st Session; H.R. 559, fn. 52. This statement by Congress adds credibility to the use of Chinese Walls in multiservice securities firms. In 1988 Congress adopted the Insider Trading and Securities Fraud Enforcement Act (Pub.L. No. 100–704 (1988)), which, among other things, amended 1934 Act § 15 to expressly require broker-dealers to set up a system of internal procedures to prevent improper misuse of nonpublic information by its employees. The 1988 legislation thus provides an express statutory mandate for the establishment of Chinese Wall or fire wall procedures.

§ 43. Execution of Customer Orders

a. *Best Execution Obligation*

Assuring fair execution of customer orders is a concern of the SEC in overseeing the operation of the securities markets. Customers can enter various types of orders. For example, a market order directs the broker (through the floor trader or market-maker) to execute the transaction at the market price. As discussed below in this section, broker-dealers have obligations to assure that customers receive a fair execution of these market orders. As an alternative to committing to purchase or sell at the market price, a customer can let the market come to him or her by placing a limit order and giving the broker specific limits. For example, a limit order would authorize purchase at a particular price or lower, but in no event higher than the price specified in the limit order. Broker-dealers have duties with regards to these orders as well. For example, there is the question of priority of limit orders. There are prohibitions against broker-dealers trading ahead of their customer's limit orders. FINRA's NASD IM–2110–2. This is designed to prevent the broker from putting its order (and therefore its interests) above that of the customer. In addition to violating trading standards, undisclosed trading ahead of customers perpetrates a deception upon those customers. This type of deception is in violation of a broker-dealer's obligations even in the absence of an express prohibition on undisclosed trading ahead of customer orders. In addition, it has been held that trading ahead of customer orders can violate state unfair trade practices prohibitions. Roskind v. Morgan Stanley Dean Witter & Co., 80 Cal.App.4th 345, 95 Cal.Rptr.2d 258 (2000).

Over the past several years, there has been increasing concern over whether brokers, especially in the OTC and NASDAQ markets, were securing the best order executions for their customers. There were charges that brokers and market-makers were conspiring on setting the spread between bid and asked quotes so as to deny customers the benefit of competitive quotes for stocks having multiple market-makers. SEC investigation of the problem led to charges of antitrust violations. On the heels of these proceedings, the SEC established a series of requirements designed to improve the execution of customer orders in the over-the-counter markets. Order Execution Obligations, 60 Fed. Reg. 52,792 (SEC 1995). The SEC adopted 1934 Act Rule 11Ac1–4, known as the "display rule." Rule 11Ac1–4 requires market-makers and specialists to display the price and the full size of customer limit orders that reflect buying and selling interest at a better price than a specialist's or market-maker's public quote. The rule also requires market-makers and specialists to increase the size of their quote for a particular security to reflect a limit order when the limit order is priced equal to the specialist's or market-maker's disseminated quote and that quote is equal to the national best bid or offer. The SEC also amended its "quote rule," which requires market-makers and specialists to publicly disseminate the best prices that they enter into an electronic communications network.

The FINRA (and formerly the NASD) continues to stress the importance of the best execution obligation. For example, the NASD announced that market-makers must show that they have written policies and procedures in place that will monitor the markets to assure that the best execution statistics that market makers report disclose are in fact correct. In 2002, the NASD sought comment on the scope of its best execution obligation. The request for comment focused on whether the best execution rule should be clarified to expressly extend to a customer order placed with one broker-dealer and then submitted to another. Further, the NASD asked for comment on another question: if the rule should be so extended to cover a correspondent firm receiving the order from the customer's broker-dealer, how the obligation should be stated.

The best execution obligation extends beyond broker-dealers. Thus, for example, investment advisers owe their customers a duty to obtain the best execution in transactions directed by the adviser. *See, e.g.,* In the Matter of Portfolio Advisory Services, Inv. Adv. Act Rel. No. IA—2038, 2002 WL 1343823 (SEC June 20, 2002) (''An investment adviser's fiduciary duty includes the requirement to seek best execution of client securities transactions''). This means that an investment adviser should ''periodically and systematically'' evaluate the execution they are receiving for their clients.

FINRA (formerly NASD) rules require brokers to use a variety of systems and procedures designed to establish the best execution. The FINRA order execution obligations are codified in FINRA (formerly NASD) Rule 2320, which provides that in any transaction for or with a customer, FINRA members and associated persons must use reasonable diligence to ascertain the best inter-dealer market for a security and buy or sell in this market in order to assure that the resulting price to the customer is as favorable as possible under prevailing market conditions. FINRA (NASD) Rule 2320(a) sets forth the following factors to be considered in the "reasonable diligence" standard: (1) the character of the market for the security, e.g., price, volatility, relative liquidity, and pressure on available communications; (2) the size and type of transaction; (3) the number of primary markets checked; and (4) the location and accessibility of primary markets and quotation sources to the customer's broker-dealer.

The FINRA and NASD interpretations and rules are also concerned with fairness in the allocation of customer orders. Although the NASD did not have a rule mandating a certain allocation system, it properly considers unfair allocation systems to be contrary to just and equitable principles of trade and therefore in violation of a broker-dealer's NASD obligations. Guidance on Compensation and Mixed Capacity Trading, Special NASD Notice to Members 01–85 (Dec. 24, 2001) (question 15). Although a system of procedures may be necessary to assure fairness in allocation of trades, the fact that the allocation is in accordance with pre-established procedures does not substitute for a case-by-case consideration of fairness.

Whether FINRA's and the NASD's order execution requirements in fact directly translate into a broker's obligation to secure the best possible execution for his or her customer has been described as "ambiguous." Newton v. Merrill Lynch, Pierce, Fenner & Smith, 115 F.3d 1127 (3d Cir. 1997), *reversed*, 30 Sec. Reg. & L. Rep. (BNA) 193 (3d Cir. 1998) (en banc). Accordingly, a three judge panel of the Third Circuit held that a broker's executions of trades only with reference to NASDAQ's National Best Bid and Offer (NBBO) electronic quotations was not actionable simply because the broker failed to disclose to the customer that the broker relied on only one quotation system and thus the trades may not have been executed at the best possible price. However, in an en banc decision, the court reinstated the claim that the broker could be held liable for executing trades at the NBBO if the broker could have secured a better execution on private on-line services such as SelectNet and Instinet. Thus, the best execution obligation defies a bright-line test. An SEC official described the obligation as executing transactions "in such a manner that the client's total cost or proceeds in each transaction is the most favorable under the circumstances." The SEC subsequently amended its display rule to require inclusion of SelectNet and Instinet quotations.

Even beyond the FINRA and NASD rules, the SEC recognizes a "best execution" obligation on the part of securities brokers. Failure to secure a good execution for the customer can be a deceptive device in violation of the securities laws' antifraud provisions. Thus, the courts have also recognized that a breach of the broker's execution obligations can constitute a material representation in violation of the antifraud provisions.

b. Confirmation of Transactions

One of the broker's obligations with respect to the execution of orders is the requirement imposed by 1934 Act Rule 10b–10 that *each* transaction be reflected in a written confirmation. Accordingly, when there are multiple transactions, there must be a confirmation for each reflecting the price for each transaction.

c. Trading Ahead of Customers

In 1994, the SEC approved an NASD rule prohibiting broker-dealers from trading ahead of their customers' limit orders. Exch. Act Rel. No. 34–34279, 1994 WL 319529 (SEC June 29, 1994) This rule expanded upon the preexisting NASD position that a market-maker could not trade ahead of a customer's limit order without first informing the customer. This rule was again expanded in May 1995 to prohibit broker-dealers from trading ahead of customer limit orders they accept from other brokers. Exch. Act Rel. No. 34–35751 60 Fed. Reg. 27,997 (SEC May 22, 1995). Accordingly, a FINRA member firm violates the rule if it accepts a customer limit order and continues to trade for its own account at a price equal to or better than the limit order unless the customer's order is filled at the limit price or better. The rule as amended also applies not only to the firm's customers but also to orders placed as member-to-member limit orders.

§ 44. Disclosure of Broker–Dealer Commissions

As mentioned above, 1934 Act Rule 10b–10 requires broker-dealers to confirm securities transactions in writing before the transaction is completed. In reality, however, the confirmation is not sent until after the investor makes the investment decision and becomes committed to the transaction. Rule 10b–10 imposes certain specific disclosure requirements in the sales confirmation. Among the disclosures required is the compensation to be received by the broker-dealer in connection with the transaction. The broker-dealer's compensation need not be disclosed in the confirmation, however, if the compensation is determined other than on a per transaction basis in accordance with a prior written agreement between the broker and the customer. 1934 Act Rule 10b–10 applies to the disclosures required in the sales confirmation. This is an after the fact disclosure obligation and does not address the disclosure obligations prior to or at the time of the transaction. In fact, Rule 10b–10 specifically admonishes that the rule does not govern the broker-dealer's obligation to make additional disclosures that may be required by the antifraud rules.

Failure to fully disclose the compensation will not only violate Rule 10b–10, but it can also form the basis of liability under 1934 Act Rule 10b–5. The fiduciary duty that a broker owes to his or her customers requires disclosure of excessive commissions. United States v. Szur, 289 F.3d 200 (2d Cir. 2002).

§ 45. Commissions, Mark–Ups, and Mark–Downs

A "commission" is the payment to a broker-dealer acting as a sales agent and usually refers to such payments for exchange transactions. "An agency trade is a trade in which a broker/dealer, authorized to act as an intermediary for the account of its customer, buys (sells) a security from (to) a third party (e.g., another customer or broker/dealer). Such a trade is not executed in, or does not otherwise pass through, the broker/dealer's proprietary account. When executing an agency trade, the broker/dealer generally charges the customer a commission for its services." Guidance on Compensation and Mixed Capacity Trading, Special NASD Notice to Members 01–85 (Dec. 24, 2001) (question 2).

Mark-ups and mark-downs consist of charges added to the transaction price and represent the way that sales commissions are generally described with respect to transactions in the over-the-counter markets.

A mark-up is the sales commission that is added to the market price of a security when a customer purchases a security. Thus, for example, if the transaction takes place at $5 per share and the broker-dealer charges a 2% mark-up, the customer will pay a total of $5.10 for each share of the security purchased, with the broker-dealer firm receiving a 10 cents per share mark-up that generally will be shared with the account executive dealing with the customer.

A mark-down is the sales commission that is deducted from the market price of a security when a customer sells a security. Thus, for example, it the transaction takes place at $5 per share and the broker-dealer charges a 2% mark-down, the customer will receive a total of $4.90 for each share of the security sold, with the broker-dealer firm receiving a 10 cents per share mark-down that generally will be shared with the account executive dealing with the customer. Note that in this context if the customer buys and sells the security at the same market price, there will be a total of 20 cents in brokerage commissions—the 10 cents per share mark-up for the purchase and the 10 cents per share markdown for the sale. It should also be noted that in an over-the-counter market there will be a spread between the bid and the asked price, meaning that a customer wanting to purchase the security will pay a higher price than the customer will receive for selling a security.

Ordinarily the terms "commission," "mark-up," and "mark-down" apply to payments to broker-dealers in connection with agency transactions. However, commissions and commission equivalent charges can also exist when the broker-dealer firm is acting in other capacities as well.

§ 46. Excessive Mark–Ups

At one time brokerage firms charged uniform commission rates. This was no longer the case as we moved into a competitive era with the abolition of fixed brokerage commission rates. The absence of fixed commission rates was designed to promote competition. With regard to exchange-traded securities, the commission is usually based on a percentage of the transaction price, or alternatively, in the case of discount brokers, at a set fee per trade or per share block. Unlike the traditional exchanges, in the OTC and NASDAQ markets, there is no centralized exchange floor and shares are traded through market-makers who purchase shares and then resell them. The difference between the bid price and asked price in the over-the-counter markets reflects a market maker's mark-up.

The charging of excessive brokerage commissions usually involves disguising all or a portion of the true mark-up that is being charged. This is a deceptive and manipulative practice that will result in disciplinary action against the offending broker-dealer.

Failure to disclose an excessive mark-up is fraudulent conduct that violates 1934 Act Rule 10b–5. Grandon v. Merrill Lynch & Co., 147 F.3d 184, 189–90 (2d Cir. 1998) In addition, excessive mark ups can form the basis of fraud and fiduciary duty claims under state law. *See, e.g.,* City of Vista v. Robert Thomas Securities, Inc., 84 Cal.App.4th 882, 101 Cal.Rptr.2d 237 (2000).

In United States v. Matthews, 2002 WL 417177 (S.D.N.Y.2002).the court indicated that nondisclosure of high commissions is not *per se* fraud is questionable, especially if taken too broadly. For example, in that particular case, the court indicated that merely "failing to disclose compensation in principal stock trades may not be criminal;" the court did not say that nondisclosure could *never* be a criminal violation. Conceivably, at some point the size of the commission becomes material to the customer in order to help judge the relationship between the customer's cost and the market price. Also, in the case of securities that are recommended by the broker, nondisclosure of a large commission can be fraudulent. As discussed in the next section, whether a broker's compensation is excessive will depend in large part on the relationship of the mark-up, mark-down, or commission to the market price. In evaluating the compensation, it is relevant to know the basis on which the broker computes the mark-up, mark down, or commission.

The SEC and SROs seek to prevent the charging of excessive commissions. For example, the SEC not only determines the types of entities that can receive remuneration from securities trades, it also imposes disclosure requirements regarding the basis of customer charges. 1934 Act Rule 10b–10. The NASD, and now FINRA, through its mark-up policy, provides guidelines as to what would constitute an excessive brokerage commission.

The Five Percent Mark–Up Policy

The NASD established a "five percent" policy as a guide for determining the fairness of the markup. This is now part of FINRA regulation. See FINRA Conduct Rules 2440, 2440–1, and accompanying interpretations. The NASD and now FINRA stress that this is a guide, not a *per se* rule or a safe harbor rule. Thus, the markup must be considered in conjunction with other factors. Some of the factors considered in determining the fairness of a mark-up are the type, availability, and price of the security, the amount of money involved in the transaction, the disclosures made to the customer, the broker-dealer's general pattern of mark-ups, and the nature of the broker-dealer's business. Mark-ups in excess of five percent are not *per se* illegal. However, the SEC has "consistently" taken the position that undisclosed mark-ups on equity securities in excess of ten percent violate the law. Thus, mark-ups in excess of ten percent are *per se* violations of the antifraud rules. See, e.g., In the Matter of Mazzeo, 2002 WL 89041 (SEC Jan. 24, 2002). The NASD takes the position that mark-ups in excess of five percent "generally" are excessive. S.E.C. v. Rauscher Pierce Refsnes, Inc., 17 F.Supp.2d 985, 998 (D.Ariz. 1998). Mark-ups below the threshold have been found to be excessive.

In computing the mark-up, the best evidence of prevailing market price is the dealer's contemporaneous cost for the securities. E.g., Lehl v. SEC, 90 F.3d 1483 (10th Cir. 1996). However, identifying the true mark-up is not always an easy task, especially in less liquid markets when there can be a time lag between a market maker's purchase of the security and its resale.

A riskless transaction occurs when a market maker simultaneously buys and sells a security or is merely matching customer orders and thus does not have any investment risk. In riskless transactions, mark-ups should be based on the cost of acquisition rather than the prevailing market price. E.g., Orkin v. SEC, 31 F.3d 1056, 1064 (11th Cir. 1994) The dealer's cost will thus be the appropriate measure of market price when faced with an integrated dealer who controls the market of the securities in question. However, in such a situation, the interdealer market is a better indicator of the true market price than the price that the integrated dealer paid in a transaction with a retail customer. The interdealer price ordinarily is the best indicator and will be rejected only when there is reason to believe that it took place in an artificially manipulated market. The fact that other dealers have accepted a security's price as established by the market maker does not eliminate the concern that the price is in fact an artificial one.

§ 47.   Payment for Order Flow

Brokers will charge other brokers a fee for directing orders to them. These payments, known as payment for order flow (see 1934 Act Rule 10b–10(d)(9)), are permissible, subject to certain disclosure requirements. Payment for order flow has long been a part of the equities markets but is a relatively new development in the options markets. Payment for order flow practices have been questioned. For example, the SEC was asked to consider barring the CBOE from permitting payment for order flow in the options markets. After considering the issue, the SEC decided to allow the practice to continue.

Nevertheless, an SEC study found that payments for order flow in the options markets does in fact have an impact on the way in which orders are routed.

The SEC has indicated that it has concerns about the practice of payment for order flow as having led to less vigorous quote competition and isolation of investor limit orders. Disclosure of Order Execution and Routing Practices, Sec. Exch. Act Rel. No. 34–43590, 2000 WL 1721163 (SEC Nov. 17, 2000) ("The Commission particularly highlighted its concerns that dealer practices such as internalization and payment for order flow have contributed to the isolation of investor limit orders and to less vigorous quote competition."). The SEC's concern is reflected in various requirements for payment for order flow. 1934 Act Rule 11Ac1–3 requires that when opening a new account, broker-dealers who will be acting as the customer's agents must make written disclosures of their policies regarding payment for order flow. The NASD has also indicated its concern with the practice and responded by requiring disclosure of payment for order flow on confirmations of customer transactions. In addition, the SEC confirmation rule, Rule 10b–10, requires disclosure of payment for order flow in transactions where the broker is acting as the customer's agent.

Directing orders pursuant to a payment for order flow arrangement can be viewed as contrary to the broker's obligation to seek the best execution for the customer. NASD Notice 01–22, 2001 WL 278615 (NASD March 16, 2001). There is considerable authority to the effect that the Securities Exchange Act preempts any fiduciary duty claims associated with failure to inform the customer of payments for order flow.

§ 48. Recommendations Induced by Commissions or Other Incentive

Even in the absence of excessive commissions, a commission structure can interfere with the impartiality of brokers in recommending securities for their customers. When a brokerage firm's commission rate structure encourages sales representatives to recommend selected securities, those recommendations will run afoul of the securities laws to the extent they are motivated by the sales representative's self interest rather than the best interests of the customer. Thus, for example, undisclosed differential sales commissions, when used as an incentive to recommend particular stocks, is a material omission from the broker's recommendation. While it is true that neither 1934 Act Rule 10b–10 nor the FINRA and NASD rules explicitly require disclosure of the compensation paid to individual brokers, when the size of the commission on selected stocks is an incentive for brokers to recommend that stock, nondisclosure is problematic. The NASD makes it clear that commissions are not limited to a portion of the transaction price charged to the customer. NASD Conduct Rule 3040 thus defines selling compensation to include any compensation that is paid directly or indirectly from whatever source as a result of the purchase or sale of a security. The definition of compensation is very broad, as the NASD "intended it to include any item of value received."

Recommendations that are induced by compensation violate the broker-dealer's obligations that generally attach to recommendations. See §§ 54–56 infra. In addition, recommendations are subject to the implied representation that brokers will deal fairly and professionally with their customers. Even beyond sales incentives, high pressure brokerage firms may unduly pressure their sales representatives to solicit transactions. The foregoing broker-dealer prohibitions are supplemented by 1933 Act § 17(b), which declares illegal the recommendation of securities for compensation without disclosing the compensation paid in connection with the making of the recommendation. A recommendation that is bought and paid for in order to promote a security violates the securities laws.

Conduct that violates 1933 Act § 17(b) ordinarily will be a violation of 1933 Act § 17(a) and 1934 Act Rule 10b–5. Accordingly, those generalized anti-fraud provisions are violated when compensation is paid to make a recommendation and the compensation is not disclosed. When a stock broker recommends a security, it is a material omission for a broker to fail to disclose to a customer that the broker had a financial interest in making the recommendation.

CHAPTER 5

MANIPULATIVE AND DECEPTIVE PRACTICES

§ 49. SEC and SRO Regulation of Broker–Dealer Conduct

There are various SEC and FINRA prohibitions addressing particular types of misconduct by broker-dealers. For example, 1934 Act Rule 15c1–2 generally prohibits fraudulent, manipulative, and deceptive practices in connection with securities brokerage transactions. Broker-dealers and their employees are also subject to 1934 Act Rule 10b–5's general antifraud proscriptions relating to deceptive conduct in connection with a purchase or sale of a security. The types of specific conduct that are addressed in other rules include market manipulation (§§ 50–52 infra), high pressure sales tactics (§ 64 infra), deceptive recommendations (§ 55 infra), generation of excessive commissions (§ 68 infra), unauthorized trading (§ 69 infra), improper order executions (§ 43 supra), improper extension of credit for securities transactions (§ 26 supra), and misuse of customer funds or securities. Beyond these specific activities and specifically identified and prohibited conduct, broker-dealers are held to just and equitable principles of trade. Further, the antifraud and anti-manipulation rules are sufficiently broad to encompass all conduct that operates as a deceptive or manipulative device in connection with securities transactions. This broad coverage thus is not limited to specific SEC rules. The SEC has taken the position in various contexts that it can regulate conduct that would be manipulative even if the concern is not based on any specified violation of existing rules. Even beyond SEC rules, the rules of the various SROs impose standards of conduct on broker-dealers. Most notably is the FINRA (formerly the NASD) general command that broker-dealers adhere to just and equitable principles of trade. Because of these general prohibitions, the specific types of misconduct that are discussed in the sections that follow do not comprise an exclusive list of the fraudulent, manipulative, and other improper broker-dealer practices.

§ 50. Prohibitions Against Deceptive and Manipulative Conduct—Prohibited Practices Generally

Because they result from artificial activity, manipulated prices are in and of themselves unfair. Conduct that is designed to artificially restrict supply is manipulative because it is designed to artificially raise prices as a result of the limited supply. Manipulative activity can consist of both fraudulent and non-fraudulent conduct.

Manipulation generally does not consist of a single act, but rather is usually accomplished through a combination of various activities. As discussed below, there are virtually an infinite variety of manipulations. However, many manipulations have a number of common characteristics. For example, the following factors frequently are "classic elements" of a market manipulation: (i) restriction of the "float" or floating supply of the securities in the public market; (ii) price leadership by the manipulator; (iii) dominating and controlling the market for the security; and (iv) a collapse of the market for the security after the manipulative activity has ceased. Fictitious trades frequently form the basis of manipulative activity. However, it is not necessary that the transactions in question be fictitious. Manipulation can infect bona fide transactions.

1934 Act Rule 15c1–2 generally prohibits fraudulent, manipulative, and deceptive practices in connection with securities brokerage transactions. Broker-dealers and their employees are also subject to the anti-manipulation provisions contained in 1934 Act §§ 9 and 10 and 1934 Act Rule 10b–5.

Sections throughout this chapter discuss various SEC, FINRA, and NASD prohibitions that address fraudulent and deceptive practices generally, as well as particular types of misconduct by broker-dealers. As discussed below, there are many rules and interpretations directed at specific manipulative practices.

At the same time, improper broker-dealer conduct is not limited to violation of SEC or SRO rules identifying specific manipulative and deceptive practices. 1934 Act Rule 10b–5 and the rules under 1934 Act § 15(c) cast a broad net over manipulative and deceptive conduct generally. Broker-dealers have an obligation to act in a professional manner and failure to do so can be a deceptive practice in violation of the generalized antifraud prohibitions. The SEC and SRO obligations outlined above may be supplemented in appropriate cases by fiduciary duty principles.

§ 51. Wash Sales, Fictitious Trades, Matched Orders, and Cross Trades

a. *Fictitious Trades*

1934 Act § 9 not only prohibits manipulative practices generally but also certain well known manipulative practices. These include wash sales, fictitious trades, and matched orders. Related to a fictitious trade is a fictitious order or "spoof" that is designed to drive the quoted price higher. Fictitious orders can also be used to artificially depress the market price of a security. By their very nature, fictitious orders are deceptive.

b. *Wash Sales*

A wash sale is a fictitious sale where there is no change in beneficial ownership of the securities. The evil of a wash sale is that it is a transaction without the usual profit motive and is designed to give the false impression of market activity when in fact there is none.

c. *Matched Orders and Cross Trades*

A matched order or cross trade occurs when orders are entered simultaneously to buy and sell the same security. The mere fact that a broker crosses trades or enters into matched orders does not violate the 1934 Act. In fact, cross trades can actually benefit the firms' customers if the savings on commissions are passed on to the customers. However, the cross trades become problematic when the cost savings are not passed on to the customer. Failure to disclose that trades entered on the customer's behalf were cross trades can constitute deceptive conduct in violation of the 1934 Act. Unauthorized cross trades also violate the securities laws. Cross trades must be recorded as such in the broker-dealer's records. See, e.g., In the Matter of Robert Schwarz, Inc., 1990 WL 310672 (SEC Aug. 31, 1990).

If the purpose of the matched order is to mislead the market or create the false impression of arm's length market activity, then the practice runs afoul of the 1934 Act's anti-manipulation provisions. Cross trades are particularly susceptible to manipulation and thus are highly "suspect" unless the broker can establish that the cross trading between accounts served a bona fide purpose.

§ 52. Other Fraudulent and Manipulative Practices

Manipulators continue to look for new ways to accomplish their nefarious ends. The following is a non-exclusive discussion of the more common types of manipulative conduct.

a. *Marking the Close*

Another type of market manipulation that can involve wash sales is "marking the close." Marking the close consists of attempting to influence a security's closing price by executing purchase or sale orders at or near the close of normal trading hours. If successful, the placing of an order to peg the price will artificially inflate or depress the closing price for the security and thus will determine the price of "market-on-close" orders placed by customers or other third parties. Marking the close manipulations can arise in several contexts. For example, marking the close is sometimes used to raise the price of a security in order to avoid a margin call at the end of the day. Downward marking the close manipulations are sometimes called "piling on," referring to piling on sales of a security in order to drive the price down. Another application of marking the close occurs when mutual funds, or investment advisers managing customer funds, enter end-of-the-day orders to artificially raise prices of securities held by the fund or managed account so that those higher prices will be reflected when the fund reports its results for the current reporting period. This is sometimes referred to as "portfolio pumping." In any context, marking the close is a serious violation.

b. *Trading Ahead of Customers*

Trading ahead of customers is an impermissible practice whereby a broker enters an order for his or her own account in advance of placing an order for customers. The object of this manipulative practice is to give the broker a preferential price. Trading ahead of customers ordinarily contravenes FINRA's and the NASD's just and equitable principles of trade. NASD IM–2110–2.

c. *Front Running*

Front running is a manipulative practice that is based on a form of insider trading. Front running exists in many forms. For example, front running can consist of trading ahead of customers' orders in order to take advantage of inside information pertaining to transactions to be entered by or on behalf of others that will have an affect on the price of the security. If the broker knows of a large sell order that will move the price downward once it is entered and executed, if the broker sells for his or her own account ahead of that order, the broker gets the advantage of the market price determined without the market's consideration of the large pending sell order. Front running is manipulative and also is inconsistent with the NASD's requirement that brokers' conduct be consistent with just and equitable principles of trade. *See* NASD IM–2110–3.

d. *Parking*

Another manipulative practice is known as parking (see § 71 infra), which consists of transferring record ownership of securities in order to hide the true identity of the beneficial owner.

e. *Free Riding*

Another deceptive practice that can take place in the context of a public offering is "free riding," which involves purchasing securities in a public offering without the intent or the funds to pay for the purchase with a view towards taking a free ride on a rising market. Free riding also violates the margin requirements that govern the extension of credit for securities transactions. In any context, entering an order to purchase a security without any intent to pay for it other than through a free ride is deceptive conduct.

f. *High Pressure Sales, Deceptive Recommendations, Excessive Commissions, Order Execution Obligations*

As noted in an earlier section, the specific fraudulent and manipulative practices that are addressed in rules include market manipulation, high pressure sales tactics (§ 64 infra), deceptive recommendations (§§ 55, 61 infra), generation of excessive commissions (§ 68 infra), unauthorized trading (§ 69 infra), improper order executions (§ 43 supra), improper extension of credit for securities transactions (§ 26 supra), and misuse of customer funds or securities.

Various manipulative practices can occur in connection with public offerings. For example, artificially preparing the market or stimulating the aftermarket will run afoul of the anti-manipulation rules. Additionally, SEC Regulation M severely restricts purchases in the course of a distribution by those persons participating in the distribution. Another manipulative practice is illegal "free riding" which involves purchasing securities in a public offering without the intent or the funds to pay for the purchase with a view towards taking a free ride on a rising market.

§ 53. Obligations of Securities Brokers

In addition to SEC rules and requirements of the applicable self-regulatory organizations, broker-dealers are subject to common law duties and some fiduciary obligations. Federal courts have recognized the existence of the fiduciary relationship in federal securities cases. See, e.g., Rolf v. Blyth Eastman Dillon & Co., Inc., 424 F.Supp. 1021, 1036 (S.D.N.Y. 1977). However, breach of a fiduciary duty will not violate the securities laws' antifraud provisions in the absence of a showing that the defendant acted with the requisite scienter. In the Matter of Flanagan, 2000 WL 98210 at *24 (SEC Initial Decision Jan. 31, 2000).

The majority view of the cases applying state common law is that a blanket fiduciary relationship between broker-dealer and client does not arise as a matter of law. (Press v. Chemical Investment Services Corp., 166 F.3d 529 (2d Cir.1999), affirming 988 F.Supp. 375, 386–87 (S.D.N.Y. 1997)). Although the majority of courts reject a blanket fiduciary duty, that additional facts can suffice to create a fiduciary duty. Id. Chief among these factors that may create a fiduciary relationship is " 'a reposing of faith, confidence and trust.' " McCracken v. Edward D. Jones & Co., 445 N.W.2d 375, 381 (Iowa App. 1989) (quoting Kurth v. Van Horn, 380 N.W.2d 693, 695 (Iowa 1986)). Such a relationship of trust and confidence may be triggered by a broker-dealer having either prior authorization to trade for the customer's account on a discretionary basis or de facto control of the account. Representing oneself to have investment and advisory expertise will give rise to fiduciary obligations. Burdett v. Miller, 957 F.2d 1375, 1381 (7th Cir. 1992). When a broker makes investment recommendations to a customer, the broker is acting in a position of trust vis a vis the customer and as such is acting as a fiduciary. United States v. Hart, 273 F.3d 363, 376 (3d Cir. 2001), relying on United States v. Hussey, 254 F.3d 428 (2d Cir. 2001).

Even in those situations where a court may recognize a fiduciary obligation, liability to the customer is not always clear. There is also a question as to the scope of the broker's duty to the customer. The SEC has referred to the "basic principle" that by holding itself out as a broker-dealer, a firm is representing that it will act in the customer's best interests. In the Matter of D.E. Wine Investments, Inc., Administrative Proceeding File No. 3–8543 Release No. ID–134, 1999 WL 373279 (SEC Initial Decision June 9, 1999), relying on Charles Hughes & Co. v. SEC, 139 F.2d 434, 436–437 (2d Cir.1943), cert. denied, 321 U.S. 786 (1944).

In reviewing the relevant state law decisions, a couple of generalizations can be made. A broker-dealer is more likely to have a duty to make a full disclosure when recommending a security, but is less likely to have an unqualified duty to provide the client with useful market information concerning the client's present portfolio even when the broker-dealer is aware of such information.

Some courts have been less vigilant in finding a fiduciary duty in the brokerage relationship. Those courts have questioned whether the common law imposes a special obligation on a broker-dealer. *See, e.g.,* Shamsi v. Dean Witter Reynolds, Inc., 743 F.Supp. 87 (D.Mass. 1989). There is considerable authority, however, to the effect that honesty and good faith are basic obligations of broker-dealers. Messer v. E.F. Hutton & Co., 833 F.2d 909, 920 (11th Cir. 1987), opinion amended on rehearing in part 847 F.2d 673 (11th Cir. 1988).

Many courts have taken the position that in a securities account where the broker does not have discretion to enter into trades or otherwise control the account's activities, the fiduciary duty is minimal, if any. DeSciose v. Chiles, Heider & Co., 239 Neb. 195, 476 N.W.2d 200 (1991), relying on Fey v. Walston & Co., Inc., 493 F.2d 1036 (7th Cir. 1974); Russo v. Bache Halsey Stuart Shields, Inc., 554 F.Supp. 613 (N.D.Ill. 1982). This is almost certain to be the case with respect to unsolicited transactions. For example, it has been said that a commodities broker in a non-discretionary account only owes the customer the duty to properly execute trades as directed by the customer (Independent Order of Foresters v. Donald, Lufkin & Jenrette, Inc., 157 F.3d 933, 940 (2d Cir. 1998) (New York law)) and that the broker does not have a further duty to call upon his or her own professional skill and prudence concerning the wisdom of any of the customer's trades. Rude v. Larson, 296 Minn. 518, 519–20, 207 N.W.2d 709, 711 (1973).

Some courts have indicated that the duties of stockbrokers are governed by federal, not state law. E.g., Smith Barney, Inc. v. Painters Local Union No. 109 Pension Fund, 254 Neb. 758, 579 N.W.2d 518 (1998). Other courts have disagreed. E.g., Levin v. Kilborn, 756 A.2d 169 (R.I. 2000). There is considerable authority to the effect that the Securities Exchange Act preempts any fiduciary duty claims associated with failure to inform the customer of payments for order flow. (See § 47 supra). Also, state law is preempted under of the Securities Litigation Uniform Standards Act of 1998 (SLUSA) (Pub. Law No. 105–353 (Nov. 3, 1998)) with respect to most securities fraud class actions involving publicly traded securities; such actions must be brought in federal court. This preemption applies to class actions brought against broker-dealers. If a suit is not brought as a class action or is brought on behalf of a class consisting of fifty or fewer class members, SLUSA's preemption does not apply.

SLUSA's preemptive effect does not extend to all broker-dealer litigation. Only class actions involving fraud in connection with the purchase or sale of a security are preempted. Thus, for example, claims based on breach of contract or breach of fiduciary duty are not preempted. Furthermore, securities fraud suits are preempted only if they are brought as a class action on behalf of more than fifty persons. Most broker-dealer litigation is not suitable for a class action since the claims are generally based on misconduct towards individual customers where the common issues of fact do not predominate.

§ 54. The Shingle Theory

A corollary to fiduciary duties is the "shingle theory," which holds that by hanging up a shingle, the broker implicitly represents that he or she will conduct business in an equitable and professional manner. A breach of the implied representation that a broker will deal fairly with the customer will be actionable under 1934 Act Rule 10b–5 only if the plaintiff can show a causal relationship between the alleged breach and an injury to the plaintiff. The shingle theory will thus be the basis of a Rule 10b–5 violation only to the extent that it amounts to a fraudulent implied misrepresentation in connection with the purchase or sale of a security.

Although often attributed to the common law, the shingle theory is well grounded under the federal securities laws as well. The shingle theory has been applied in both SEC enforcement actions and private damage actions under the federal securities laws.

The shingle theory arose in the context of brokers' charging excessive mark-ups, but it is not limited to mark-up cases. Charles Hughes & Co. v. SEC, 139 F.2d 434 (2d Cir. 1943), cert. denied 321 U.S. 786 (1944). When brokers hold themselves out as experts either in investments in general or in the securities of a particular issuer, they will be held to a higher standard of care in making recommendations. In applying this aspect of shingle theory, a broker who makes a recommendation is viewed as making an implied representation that he or she has adequate information on the security in question for forming the basis of the broker's opinion. This concept of implied representation has also been expressed in terms of a broker-dealer "implicitly warrant[ing] the soundness of the statements of stock value," (Kahn v. SEC, 297 F.2d 112, 115 (2d Cir. 1961) (Clark J., concurring)) but this is too strong a statement of the rule. The concept of implied warranty has not to date been extended to brokers' recommendations and the appropriate standard of care whether under the shingle theory or otherwise is necessarily based upon the broker-dealer's factual basis and reasonable belief in the opinions that form the basis of the recommendation.

The shingle theory can be used in many contexts. For example, in judging the appropriate standard of care that attaches to a broker-dealer in recommending securities to his or her customers and in dealing with the customers' accounts generally, the Commission has relied upon the "shingle theory." The shingle theory is but an extension of the common law doctrine of "holding out." It has long been established that since the broker occupies a special position of trust and confidence with regard to his or her customer, any recommendation of a security carries with it an implicit representation that the broker has an adequate basis for the recommendation. E.g., Hanly v. SEC, 415 F.2d 589, 596 (2d Cir. 1969).

§ 55. Recommendations Generally; Know the Security Obligation

The existence of the broker-customer relationship establishes special duties whenever a broker recommends a security. The securities laws prohibit a broker-dealer from recommending a security unless he or she has actual knowledge of the characteristics and fundamental facts relevant to the security in question; furthermore, the recommendation must be reasonably supported by the facts. This is sometimes referred to as the "know the security" obligation. As noted previously, there is an implied representation that the broker is informed as to the security and that the recommendation has a reasonable factual basis.

The securities laws prohibit a broker-dealer from recommending a security unless he or she has actual knowledge of the characteristics and fundamental facts relevant to the security in question; furthermore, the recommendation must be reasonably supported by the facts. This is but one example of the way in which existence of the broker-customer relationship can establish special duties with regard to the securities broker. In the context of a securities brokerage relationship, whenever a broker recommends a security to a customer, there is an implied representation that the broker is informed as to the security and that the recommendation has a reasonable factual basis. When a broker recommends a security for purchase there is said to be an implied representation that the broker "has made a thorough investigation." See, e.g., Alton Box Bd. Co. v. Goldman, Sachs & Co., 560 F.2d 916, 922 (8th Cir. 1977). The obligation to have a basis for the recommendation sometimes is referred to as the "know the security" obligation. The broker's responsibilities do not end with this obligation. Consideration must also be given to whether the broker has a conflict of interest when making the recommendation. A broker's or securities analyst's recommendation should not be unduly influenced by special incentives from the brokerage firm or from others. This obligation is sometimes referred to as the "know your security" obligation. It also is sometimes called "reasonable basis suitability."

§ 56. Suitability Generally

In addition to the broker-dealer's knowledge of the security, there are also obligations imposed with regard to the broker-dealer's duty to know his or her customer. The SEC has not established suitability requirements applicable to broker-dealers generally, but such an obligation can be found in the rules of the self-regulatory organizations. Although the SEC imposes a suitability requirement on certain penny stock recommendations (1934 Act Rules 15g–1 et seq), there has not to date been an expansion of this requirement except with respect to so-called penny stocks (see § 59 infra).

A violation of the SRO rules, without more, will not provide an independent basis for private relief by an injured investor, although it may be relevant in an action brought under 1934 Act Rule 10b–5. The essence of a Rule 10b–5 claim is deception, which generally means misrepresentation or nondisclosure. A broker's recommendation of a security will give rise to damages to the customer for an unsuitable recommendation only if the recommendation contains an express or implied material misrepresentation of the risks involved. As explained by one court: "the plaintiff asserting unsuitability must show (1) the investment was incompatible with the plaintiff's investment objectives; and (2) the broker recommended the investment although (3) the broker knew or reasonably believed the investment was inappropriate." Keenan v. D.H. Blair & Co., 838 F.Supp. 82, 87 (S.D.N.Y. 1993).

§ 57. SRO Suitability Obligations

a. NASD Suitability Rule

The NASD, and now FINRA, in its so-called "suitability rule" requires that in recommending a purchase or sale of a particular security to a customer, the broker-dealer must have "reasonable grounds for believing that the recommendation is suitable for such customer upon the basis of the facts, if any, disclosed by such customer as to his other security holdings and as to his financial situation and needs." FINRA Rule 2310. Interestingly, the suitability rule on its face does not impose upon the broker any affirmative duty of investigating the customer's investment objectives but merely requires the broker-dealer to act reasonably based upon the information, if any, that the customer provides. Nevertheless, the NASD in a policy statement by its Board of Governors goes further by requiring the broker to obtain information concerning the customers' other securities holdings before recommending speculative, low priced securities.

The suitability and know-your-customer obligations have arisen in the context of broker-dealer recommendations. There has been some suggestion that the concept should be extended to the broker's suggested obligation to monitor the investor's own decisions. However, there is considerable authority to the contrary, holding that the broker does not have a duty to intercede when the investment is the customer's choice rather than the basis of the broker's recommendation.

The NASD indicated that the suitability obligation can exist with regard to institutional investors. Under the NASD interpretation there are two important considerations in invoking the suitability doctrine for institutional investors. The first consideration is the institutional customer's ability to comprehend and evaluate independently the risks involved. The second factor is the extent to which the customer will be exercising independent judgment in evaluating the recommendation. Suitability rules regarding recommendations to institutional investors are especially timely in light of many crises involving derivative investments. Banca Cremi, S.A. v. Alex. Brown & Sons, Inc., 132 F.3d 1017 (4th Cir. 1997).

The Municipal Securities Rulemaking Board has a suitability requirement that applies to recommendations of municipal securities to non-institutional investors. MSRB Rule G–19. In addition, the SEC imposes a suitability requirement for the extension of credit outside of FRB Reg. T when credit is extended in connection with securities transactions.

b. NYSE Know–Your–Customer Rule

In addition to the NASD's suitability rule, NYSE Rule 405 expressly imposes obligations on broker-dealers. Rather than talk in terms of suitable investments, the NYSE expressly places upon member broker-dealers an affirmative obligation to "know-your-customer" with regard to sales or offers as well as recommendations.

c. FINRA and Recommendations

As can be seen from the discussion that follows, the FINRA suitability requirements in large part follow those previously adhered to by the NASD. The know your security (see § 56 above) and suitability obligations are now incorporated into FINRA's regulatory scheme. In 2010 the SEC approved a consolidated, FINRA rule to replace the former NASD suitability and NYSE know-your-customer rules. The new FINRA Rule accomplishes three things. First, FINRA Rule 2111 codifies the "reasonable basis" (or know your security) obligation by providing that in making a recommendation with respect to a security, the firm must have a reasonable basis for believing, based on a due diligence investigation, that the recommendation is suitable for at least some investors. Second, the FINRA rule includes a reasonable basis suitability standard by requiring that the firm must have reasonable grounds to believe that a recommendation is suitable for the specific investor to whom the recommendation is made. Third, there is a quantitative approach to recommendations in that the rule requires that firms have a reasonable basis for believing that the number of recommended transactions with a certain time frame is not excessive. This quantitative limitation is aimed at helping to prevent churning and excessive trading issues.

Applying suitability standards. From time to time, the NASD identified investments that are particularly susceptible to suitability concerns. For example, the NASD targeted online trading and day trading, low priced securities, and mutual fund sales practices. Additionally, in a notice to members, the NASD issued a reminder of suitability obligations as they related to hedge fund recommendations. The NASD also issued an interpretation applying its suitability rule to advice given institutional investors. As noted earlier, under the NASD interpretation there are two important considerations in invoking the suitability doctrine for institutional investors. The first consideration is the institutional customer's ability to comprehend and independently evaluate the risks involved. The second factor is the extent to which the customer will be exercising independent judgment in evaluating the recommendation.

No duty to protect customers from themselves. Consistent with the approach taken by the NASD, FINRA's suitability and know-your-customer obligations have arisen in the context of broker-dealer recommendations. There has been some suggestion that the concept should be extended to the broker's suggested obligation to monitor the investor's own decisions. However, there is considerable authority to the contrary, holding that the broker does not have a duty to intercede when the investment is the customer's choice rather than on the basis of the broker's recommendation. See § 63 below.

§ 58.   Purported "Dram Shop" Liability and the Financial Suicide Cases

Borrowing its name from the statutes imposing liability on tavern owners for serving too much alcohol to their customers, a new variety of customer claims based on a "dram shop" theory of liability has arisen in broker-dealer arbitration and customer initiated litigation. As discussed in the preceding subsections, the suitability obligation arises in the context of the broker's recommending securities to the customer. It does not impose an obligation to protect the customer from his or her own folly with respect to unsolicited trades. However, there have been a number of arbitration complaints based on just such an obligation. Typically, in these "dram shop" obligations, the claim is that the broker-dealer had an obligation to protect customers from their own investment decisions resulting in unsolicited transactions—namely, not involving securities recommended by the broker. These claims have alternatively been described as the "financial suicide" cases. This would be a clear expansion of the decisions and administrative interpretations that developed the suitability doctrine. The possibility of courts recognizing this expansion scares brokers since it is contrary to the traditional rule that in unsolicited transactions, brokers owe customers only minimal duties. It seems clear that the mere existence of a brokerage relationship does not put the broker under an obligation to prevent the customer from committing financial suicide. See de Kwiatkowski v. Bear, Stearns & Co., Inc., 306 F.3d 1293 (2d Cir. 2002) (overturning $111.5 million jury award). However, fiduciary duties are created when a broker undertakes the responsibility to monitor the account or when the broker exercises discretion over the account.

§ 59. Special Suitability Problems Associated With Low Priced Securities

There has been increasing concern over low priced securities that are not marketed through a national exchange or the NASD national market system. Many investors have been injured as a result of high pressure sales techniques in connection with these so-called "penny stocks." In response, in 1989, the Commission proposed special regulation of penny stocks. Under the proposed rule, cold calls were to be outlawed and sales could not be completed unless the customer had first signed a written agreement. Furthermore, before executing a sale for a customer, a broker would have to determine that the securities were a suitable investment for the customer. The determination of suitability would have to be documented. The proposed rule evidenced the SEC's position that penny stocks are not suitable for many investors. The penny stock regulations were implemented in 1990 and expanded in 1992. The advent of these regulations was seen as having implications beyond penny stocks insofar as the Commission would be expressly recognizing a suitability obligation not heretofore contained in SEC rules. This has proved to be the case. Congress codified the penny stock obligations. 1934 Act § 15(g).

§ 60. Suitability and Mutual Fund Sales Practices

Mutual funds are generally considered to be long-term investments. Recommendations regarding frequent switching of mutual funds can run afoul of the NASD's suitability requirements. For similar reasons, recommendations calling for frequent switching of variable annuity investments are not proper.

In 1995, the NASD issued a directive concerning the obligations of member broker-dealers with respect to mutual fund sales practices. NASD Notice to Members 95–80 (Sept. 26, 1995). There is an obligation to assure that when recommending mutual funds all material facts are disclosed to investors. Material facts include the fund's investment objectives, portfolio, performance history, expense ratio, and sales charges. The risks of investing in the recommended fund as compared with other investment products are also material and must be disclosed.

§ 61. Suitability and Investment Advisers

In 1994, the SEC proposed a rule that would expressly prohibit an investment adviser from making recommendations of securities that are unsuitable for his or her clients. However, that rule was never adopted. In light of the proposal not having been adopted, the only formal suitability requirement would be the one that is recognized with regard to broker-dealer recommendations. Nevertheless, the SEC has taken the position that the antifraud provisions of the Investment Advisers Act can be used to enforce a suitability requirement. See MLC Limited, 1997 WL 408759 n. 2 (SEC No Action Letter July 21, 1997).

§ 62. Recommendations and Conflicts of Interest; Analysts' Recommendations

Another problem that arises in connection with securities recommendations is nondisclosure of potential conflicts of interest. It is improper for any person to recommend a security for the purposes of enhancing the value of one's own investments in that security. See § 63 infra. In addition, it is impermissible to receive compensation for making a recommendation of a particular security without disclosing that compensation. 1933 Act § 17(b). According to the "know the security" obligation, when making a recommendation, there is an obligation to have a reasonable basis for the recommendation. See § 55 supra.

Particular conflict of interest problems arise in connection with recommendations by brokerage firms' research departments. For example, when the firm provides investment banking services to a company, its research recommendations with respect to that company may be compromised. The Chinese Wall, fire wall, or information barrier (see § 42 supra) has not been sufficient in insulating security analysts from conflicts of interest.

In response to several scandals involving analyst recommendations, the NASD moved to require analysts making public recommendations to disclose any ownership positions they may have in the securities being recommended. This proposal was criticized as not going far enough in addressing securities analysts' potential conflicts of interests. Subsequently, the NASD announced a set of proposed rules for analysts' recommendations. Exch. Act Rel. No. 34–45526, 2002 WL 389246 (SEC March 14, 2002). The SEC approved these rules, which are in large measure a codification of existing NASD rules and interpretations regarding the implications to be drawn from preexisting rules addressing fair practice and disclosure obligations. The NASD rules on analysts' recommendations make more explicit the requirements that have traditionally been imposed under the more generalized requirements that NASD members adhere to just and equitable principles of trade. The NASD specifically addressed analysts' compensation, the relationship between a firm's investment banking and research departments, the personal trading activities of analysts, and disclosures relating to the firm's and the analyst's ownership of securities. The rules also impose a quiet period on recommendations following a firm's underwriting activities. The NASD proposal was drafted in consultation with the New York Stock Exchange, which agreed to impose similar requirements upon its members.

The NASD and now FINRA rules explicitly provide that an analyst's compensation may not be tied to specific investment banking transactions. Furthermore, if the analyst's compensation is based in any degree upon the investment banking revenues, the research reports must disclose this. Disclosure is also required if the firm or its affiliates received compensation from that company within the previous 12 months; disclosure is also required if the firm or affiliates expect to receive compensation from the company within the next three months following publication of the report. Additionally, when an analyst recommends a security in a public appearance, the analyst must disclose if the issuer is a client of the firm.

The requirements regarding analysts' independence preclude a research analyst from being supervised or controlled by a firm's investment banking department. The research department must act independently of the investment banking department and may only have reports checked for factual accuracy by either the investment banking department or the company that is the subject of the report.

The independence requirements preclude an analyst or member of the analyst's household from purchasing or receiving a company's securities prior to its IPO if the company is engaged in the same business that the analyst follows and issues reports about. The rules also impose a trading moratorium so that no analyst or household member may trade securities issued by companies the analyst follows for thirty days prior to the issuance of the research report and ending five days after the date of the research report. The rules also prohibit analysts and household members from making trades contrary to the analyst's most current recommendations.

The FINRA (formerly NASD) rules require that when making a public appearance an analyst must disclose (and a firm must disclose in research reports) if the analyst or a household member has a financial interest in the securities of a recommended company. Any other known conflict of interest must also be disclosed in the research report or during the public appearance. Additionally, if a firm, as of five business days before the public appearance or publication of a research report, owns one percent or more of any equity class of the company, there must be disclosure in the research report or during the appearance.

The FINRA (and formerly NASD) rules also impose a quiet period for securities offerings registered under the 1933 Act where the analyst's firm participates as an underwriter. The rules as proposed and adopted require quiet periods during which a firm acting as manager or co-manager of a securities offering may not issue a report on a company within forty days after an initial public offering or within ten days after a secondary offering. The rules also prohibit a firm from offering or threatening to withhold favorable research to induce business.

The SEC further has indicated that the new NASD (FINRA) rules on analysts' conflicts of interest may only be a "first step" in increased efforts to deal with the problem. For example, the SEC announced that it was considering requiring brokerage firms to spin-off their research departments. While this has not come to pass, analyst conflicts of interest remain a pressing problem.

New York took the lead in pursuing analysts' conflicts of interest as evidenced by its pursuit of high profile brokerage firms. For example, Merrill Lynch agreed in a settlement with the New York Attorney General to create a Web site to list all of its relevant banking relationships with companies discussed in its research reports in the preceding twelve months and also to include this same information directly in its research reports. Additionally, Merrill Lynch agreed to state on the cover of every research report that investors should assume the firm is seeking, or will seek, investment banking business from the covered company. Following on the heels of the actions of the New York Attorney

General, the SEC announced that it was investigating problems relating to analysts' recommendations and conflicts of interest.

In the Sarbanes–Oxley Act of 2002 (Pub. Law 107–204 (July 30, 2002)), which deals primarily with corporate and accounting fraud, Congress mandated that the SEC promulgate rules addressing the conduct of firms with research analysts. The 2002 amendments contain provisions to preserve the objectivity of research analysts by enhancing the separation between investment bankers and research analysts. The Act further mandated SEC rulemaking regarding disclosures relating to potential analysts' conflicts.

§ 63. Scalping

A fraudulent practice that has been utilized by some unscrupulous investment advisers and securities dealers is known as "scalping." Scalping consists of an investment adviser's purchasing a security in advance of making a buy recommendation, with the knowledge that a buy recommendation will help drive up the price of the stock. The stock is sold at a profit once the scalper's recommendation has been issued and the price has risen in reaction thereto.

In SEC v. Capital Gains Research Bureau, Inc., 375 U.S. 180 (1963), the Supreme Court held that failure to disclose an intention to scalp operates as a fraud or deceit upon an investment adviser's prospective clients under the terms of ICA § 206. The Court ruled that the concept of fraud or deceit in section 206 of the Act is not limited to material misstatements but also extends to omissions of material fact. The Court explained: "The high standards of business morality exacted by our laws regulating the securities industry do not permit an investment adviser to trade on the market effect of his own recommendations without fully and fairly revealing his personal interest(s) in these recommendations to his clients." The evil involved with scalping is based on the making of recommendations without disclosing the conflict of interest arising out of the shares owned by the person making the recommendation.

Scalping is not limited to investment adviser activity and also violates 1934 Act Rule 10b–5. Zweig v. Hearst Corp., 594 F.2d 1261 (9th Cir. 1979). Scalping also violates the rules of self-regulatory organizations such as the national exchanges and FINRA.

As noted in § 48 supra, 1933 Act § 17(b) outlaws practices similar to scalping. 1933 Act § 17(b) prohibits the making of a recommendation to sell a security without disclosing any compensation that may have been paid to the person making the recommendation. Section 17(b) is aimed at preventing the misleading impression of impartiality in certain recommendations. Section 17(b)'s prohibitions were "particularly designed to meet the evils of the 'tipster sheet,' as well as articles in newspapers or periodicals that purport to give an unbiased opinion but which in reality are bought and paid for." However, the anti-touting provisions have been applied equally to broker-dealers and others.

§ 64. High Pressure Sales Tactics; Boiler Rooms and Bucket Shops

In making his or her recommendation to the customer, the broker-dealer is under an obligation not only to know and consider the customer's investment objectives but also to have some familiarity with the security being recommended. (See §§ 54, 55 supra). One unfortunate practice that has developed with some of the more unscrupulous securities brokers and dealers is a concerted high pressure sales campaign that frequently includes the cold calling of individuals who are not regular customers. Brokerage firms sponsoring such high pressure sales campaigns typically pressure their sales representatives to push the securities in question through the use of sales incentives or other tactics.

The movie "Boiler Room" (New Line Cinema (2000)) accurately depicted many of the tactics used in the perpetration of securities brokers' high pressure sale frauds. The extreme measures portrayed in that movie were not an exaggeration. In fact, they reflect many of the tactics found in the SEC and NASD decisions. These tactics are not new. In fact, similar overreaching brokerage sales programs were behind the regulation that Congress imposed in 1934. For example, many of these operations "lent a carnival tone to securities marketing." Joel Seligman, The Transformation of Wall Street 24

(1982). In particular, Congress was concerned with sales contests for brokers, awarding liberal prizes to the brokers and/or offices with the most securities sales. These types of sales campaigns are thus clearly inconsistent with the just and equitable principles of trade that apply to securities brokers under the 1934 Act and system of self-regulation that exists thereunder. Conduct that may be acceptable in other sales intensive businesses simply is not to be tolerated for securities brokers. High pressure sales operations often result in criminal convictions and imprisonment. Injured investors have been able to recover damages in broker-dealer arbitration proceedings.

High pressure sales schemes or boiler room operations consist of various nefarious practices, any one of which standing alone constitutes a violation of the securities laws. Thus, although it is common to find these tactics grouped together, it is not necessary to find such a pattern in order to invoke the sanctions of the securities laws and the self-regulatory system. Boiler room operations have resulted in successful criminal prosecutions.

In a typical boiler room operation, callers recommend purchases of large blocks of speculative securities in new companies, predicting dramatic earnings and rapid increases in the market prices of the securities. Technology has expanded boiler rooms beyond telecommunications as the Internet has become a fertile medium for securities fraud. It has been observed that "[i]n the old days, you had the boiler rooms where you had to hire 20 people to make thousands of phone calls to sell fraudulent securities. Now one person can do this by the push of a button." Debate in Senate on H.R. 1058 Reported by Conference Committee (2000) (James B. Adelman, former head of enforcement of the SEC's Boston office).

Sometimes the term "bucket shop" is used interchangeably with "boiler room." The bucket shop has many of the same high pressure sales tactics as a boiler room but has a different history. The "bucket shops" that operated long ago were based on a failure to enter customer orders on an exchange and thus turning the apparent transactions into illegal difference contracts or simply wagers. The term bucket shop is based on the facts that customer orders were thrown in a bucket rather than executed in the markets. The essence of the bucket shop is the fictitious nature of the transactions. In contrast, boiler rooms use high pressure sales with respect to real transactions that actually take place. Bucket shops and boiler room operations as high pressure sales campaigns are inconsistent with the broker-dealer's implied representation under the shingle theory to conduct its business in a professional (i.e. just and equitable) manner.

In the context of a boiler room, high pressure sales campaigns can constitute securities fraud and illegal manipulative activity. Thus, for example, boiler room activities and other high pressure sales tactics can violate 1934 Act Rule 10b–5 and can also form the basis for NASD disciplinary sanctions. One benchmark of the boiler room variety of high pressure sales tactics is heavy reliance on telephone solicitations and usually concentrating on long-distance cold calling operations. Another common high pressure tactic that implicates the anti-manipulation rules is the use of prewritten scripts, including prepared rebuttals to customer objections. This is often accompanied by high commissions to sales representatives for pushing the stocks in question. Many boiler room type operations routinely use unregistered sales representatives. Frequently, boiler room operations involve shell companies or other scam stocks.

Brokers and others who sell securities often are very aggressive in their marketing techniques. However, not every instance of high pressure sales tactics will violate the securities laws. Material misrepresentations and omissions can of course expose brokers and others to potential liabilities under the securities laws, but high pressure sales tactics alone will not rise to the requisite level of fraud. On the other hand, when brokers and brokerage firms cross the line between permissible accepted sales tactics and impermissible manipulative or deceptive conduct, they can be held accountable for this conduct under the securities laws.

A common manipulative device is for a brokerage firm to compensate brokers in such a way as to encourage high pressure sales. Such differential commissions violate the antifraud provisions and the FINRA's (NASD's) just and equitable principles of trade. In extreme cases, customer sell orders may even be ignored.

One of the features of a boiler room operation is an aggressive cold calling program whereby a broker calls someone with whom there has been no prior business relationship and tries to enlist him or her as a client. The practice of cold calling has not been limited to boiler room operations and has been utilized by many of the more established retail brokerage firms. In 1994, Congress enacted the Telemarketing and Consumer Fraud and Abuse Prevention Act (Pub. L. No. 103–297 (1994)). Both the NYSE and NASD developed rules requiring member firms to maintain and preserve "do not call lists." Among other things, the rules require firms to honor requests not to be called by the firm or its sales agents. The rules also contain sanctions for violations of the requirement that a list be maintained and also for failure to honor customers' requests to be left alone. Many states have their own telemarketing laws that supplement the federal law and in some cases go further.

§ 65. Manipulation of IPOs

Sometimes high pressure sales tactics are used in connection with public offerings that would be manipulative and deceptive. For example, a brokerage firm might unduly encourage its registered representatives to encourage customer purchases by giving higher commissions to sales representatives for transactions where the customer purchases rather than sells the securities in question. Especially if undisclosed to the customer, this type of compensation for trades encourages the creation of more purchases than sales. Another practice is to pre-sell the offering in the after-market. This manipulation is carried out when broker-dealers require or encourage customers to commit to purchasing shares in the after-market in order to get part of the allotment out of the original issue. This, of course, generates additional after-market buying activity that is manipulative in that it is designed to push the price higher once the security comes to market. In addition, when broker-dealers combine public offerings with "boiler room" or other improper high pressure sales tactics, they are engaging in deceptive and manipulative conduct since these activities precondition the after-market following an initial offering.

§ 66. Pump & Dump Schemes

Another variation of high pressure sales tactics frequently associated with boiler rooms and other manipulations are "pump and dump" schemes. Pump and dump operations often involve high pressure recommendations, withholding securities from the market and other manipulative actions designed to inflate a security's price before the manipulator dumps those shares on the market. Pump and dump schemes have also been carried out over the Internet whereby people use a chat room or other means of online communication to "talk up" a particular security before dumping shares by selling them on unsuspecting investors.

§ 67. Microcap Fraud

In the 1990s, "microcap" fraud stole the forefront from the penny stock problems of the late 1980s and early 1990s. Microcap is the new term used for very small capitalization companies. The Internet has been used for many microcap offerings and has led to several abuses and securities law violations. In 1999, the SEC amended 1933 Act Rule 504 to prohibit the use of the exemption from 1933 Act registration for public offerings unless they are registered or exempt under state law.

In another move designed to focus on microcap securities, the SEC proposed amending 1934 Act Rule 15c2–11 to require broker-dealers to review information about a company before it initiates quotations for unlisted over-the-counter securities. Although the proposed amendment to the rule was not adopted, the NASD decided to monitor microcap offerings to determine if implementation of the proposal is necessary. In 2002, the NASD formally proposed, and subsequently adopted, a rule requiring the broker to review specified information before making recommendations in securities that are not traded on NASDAQ or through some other electronic quotations medium. *See* Order Approving Proposed Rule Change and Notice of Filing and Order Granting Accelerated Approval to Amendment No. 2 to the Proposed Rule Change by the National Association of Securities Dealers, Inc. Relating to Microcap Initiative—Recommendation Rule, Sec. Exch. Act Rel. No. 34–46376, 67 Fed. Reg. 54832–01, 2002 WL 1949161 (SEC Aug. 26, 2002); Proposed NASD Rule 2315, File No. SR–NASD–99–04, Sec. Exch. Act Rel. No. 34–45277 (SEC Jan. 14, 2002). See FINRA Rule 2114.

§ 68. Churning

1934 Act Rule 15c1–7 prohibits excessive trading by a broker for any account in which he or she holds discretionary trading powers. When a broker in a discretionary trading account enters into transactions for the purpose of generating commissions, the broker unjustifiably gains from the customer's loss or transaction costs. This practice is generally referred to as "churning" the customer's account. Rule 15c1–7 declares churning to be a "manipulative, deceptive or other fraudulent device or contrivance." The SEC rule is limited by its terms to trading accounts where the broker has the discretion to enter into transactions, but the account overall need not be formally discretionary.

Churning does not always involve a discretionary account and can arise when the broker exercises de facto control. A 1949 SEC ruling took the position that the "handling of a customer's account may become fraudulent whenever the broker or dealer is in a position to determine the volume and frequency of transactions by reason of the customer's willingness to follow the suggestions of the broker or the dealer and he abuses the customer's confidence by overtrading." In re Norris & Hirshberg, 21 S.E.C. 865, 890 (1946), affirmed sub nom. Norris & Hirshberg v. SEC, 177 F.2d 228 (D.C.Cir. 1949). Churning, de facto or otherwise, violates the 1934 Act general antifraud provisions.

Churning claims are sometimes accompanied by claims that the investments were unsuitable for the investor and thus violated the suitability rules. In fact, the mere existence of excessive trades based on a broker's recommendations can violate the suitability requirements.

In order to establish churning, it is generally necessary to prove substantial disparity between the turnover in the account in question and the normal trading activity for similar accounts. For example, in one case the plaintiff prevailed by showing that an account that amounted to less than one-tenth of one percent of the local office's portfolio value generated 4.7 percent of its commission income. Although the damaging turn-over rate must necessarily be decided on a case by case basis, it appears that a given account's annual turn-over rate in excess of six times is considered generally to reflect excessive trading. In addition, a court will review the patterns of trading; for example, courts should scrutinize sales soon after or at the same time as purchases (or purchases soon after sales) of the same security, where one account buys a particular security just as another sells, as well as looking at the commissions and profits of the broker with regard to the transactions under scrutiny. In such cases, where one or more of these factors are present, the burden would presumably shift to the broker to justify this activity.

The types of investments being made will also be relevant to the determination of whether there has been excessive trading. Ordinarily, less of a turnover rate will be tolerated in debt investments than in equity holdings. Similarly, a higher turnover rate ordinarily will be permitted in options as opposed to equity transactions. As noted earlier, an important element of any churning claim is establishing that the defendant had control of the account and the power to trade.

One problem that frequently arises in the churning context is the extent to which the culpable broker-dealer's employer will be held accountable for a registered representative's churning activities. Liability of the employer may be asserted under either a variation of the common law doctrine of *respondeat superior* or 1934 Act § 20(a)'s liability of controlling persons. See § 76 infra.

The appropriate measure of damages is not always easy to identify in a churning case. The general rule appears to be that the defendant is liable only for the losses due to the excessive commissions plus accrued interest. Hecht v. Harris, Upham & Co., 430 F.2d 1202 (9th Cir. 1970). However, some courts have assessed the measure of damages as the excess of the average decline in market values over the decline in value of the plaintiff's portfolio. *E.g.* Miley v. Oppenheimer & Co., 637 F.2d 318 (5th Cir. 1981).

Since the evil involved is the generation of excessive commissions, the fact that the customer's account increased in value does not preclude a churning claim. Davis v. Merrill Lynch, Pierce, Fenner & Smith, Inc., 906 F.2d 1206 (8th Cir. 1990); Nesbit v. McNeil, 896 F.2d 380 (9th Cir. 1990).

§ 69.   Unauthorized Trading

An unauthorized trade is simply the purchase or sale of stock by a broker on behalf of a customer who has not authorized the transaction. Unauthorized trading claims can arise in many contexts. The only defense to unauthorized trading claims is that the broker in fact had the authority or discretion to execute the transactions in question. The broker can get such authority from a specific customer order or from a grant of discretionary trading authority. Grants of discretionary trading authority require prior written authorization. Specifically, FINRA (formerly NASD) Rule of Conduct 2510 provides that a registered representative may not exercise discretionary trading authority without written authorization. Unauthorized trading claims have also arisen in connection with liquidation of margin positions, but authorization for these liquidations ordinarily is included in the customer's margin agreement.

Unauthorized trading differs from churning in that under a churning claim, the plaintiff will attempt to show that excessive trading has occurred on his account simply to generate brokerage fees or commissions. The plaintiff in churning cases need not argue that the trading was *per se* unauthorized. Usually, the customer authorizes trading on his or her account; the evil in churning cases is the broker's excessive trading in order to generate commissions. A variation on unauthorized trading is the ignoring of customer sell orders. This obviously is not to generate sales commissions but rather may be part of a scheme to manipulate and thereby inflate the price of the stock in question.

Unauthorized trading is not *per se* a violation of 1934 Act Rule 10b–5. "[A]n unauthorized trade does not violate the antifraud provisions of the Securities Exchange Act unless it is accompanied by an intent to defraud or a willful and reckless disregard of the client's best interests." Messer v. E.F. Hutton & Co., 833 F.2d 909, 917 (11th Cir. 1987), opinion amended on rehearing in part, 847 F.2d 673 (11th Cir. 1988).

Even in those cases where the unauthorized trading alone is not actionable under the federal securities laws, such conduct may form the basis of a claim for breach of contract or breach of fiduciary duty. Similarly, an unauthorized sale of the plaintiff's stock may be actionable under the common law theory of conversion.

§ 70. Regulation of Short Sales

If an investor believes that the price of a security is likely to decline, there are several potential investment strategies. Most such strategies are linked to dealing with put and call options. Another alternative is to enter an order to sell the security at the current price with the understanding that the investor is to fulfill that obligation at a later date by purchasing the security at a lower price on a later date. In order to make a profit from this transaction the investor must be able to buy the security at a price lower than that at which he or she previously sold the security. This practice of selling stock without actually owning it is known as selling short. Selling short, is extremely risky since every increase in the price causes loss to the investor until he or she covers the short sale. An alternative method is "selling against the box," where securities are borrowed as collateral for delivery for sale at a later date.

The mechanics of a short sale are as follows. The customer borrows the security from the broker in order to be able to deliver the securities to the purchaser in the short sale transaction. In turn, the customer pays interest on the loan until he or she closes the transaction by purchasing the securities in question and restores that stock to the broker. As pointed out above, an alternative method to effectuate the transaction is known as "selling against the box," where rather than borrow securities from the broker, he or she uses securities that he or she already owns as collateral for the short sale. When the customer posts collateral for the short sale or sale against the box, the brokerage firm may earn profits from the collateral so held. Failure to inform the customer of these profits is not securities fraud. Levitin v. PaineWebber, Inc., 159 F.3d 698 (2d Cir. 1998).

Because of the speculative nature of and potential for abuse associated with short sales and sales against the box, insiders of publicly traded securities are strictly prohibited from engaging in such transactions. 1934 Act § 16(c). Also, short sales are not meant for the ordinary investor both because of the risk involved and the level of sophistication that should exist before an investor embarks upon such a transaction.

Because of the risky nature of a short sale investment strategy, a broker has a duty to explain the transaction in a manner understandable to the investor. Vucinich v. Paine, Webber, Jackson & Curtis, Inc., 803 F.2d 454 (9th Cir. 1986). This is equally true of a short position in options.

Short selling has the potential to be manipulative and can be used as part of a scheme to manipulate the market. However, short selling by itself is not manipulative. The fact that there is a large amount of short selling that necessarily has the effect of depressing a stock's price does not make the short sales manipulative. The key question in any manipulation case is not whether the activity in fact affected the price of the stock but whether the activity was entered into for the purpose of affecting the price.

The SEC has regulated short sales since 1938. 1934 Act Rule 10a–1 applied to short sale transactions with regard to securities on a national securities exchange and requires that a short sale not be entered below the last sales price. Furthermore, the short sale cannot be at the last sale price "unless such price is above the next preceding different price." Rule 10a–1 thus required that short sale transactions be entered on a volume-weighted price basis. In 1994, the SEC approved NASD rules that impose a "bid-test" rule for short sale transactions. The NASD rules prohibited broker-dealers from effecting a short sale for themselves or their customers if the short sale bid is lower than the previous inside bid. The rule went on to exempt certain transactions from the prohibition on "down bids." In order to comply with the NASD rule when the current inside bid is a "down bid," the short sale must be at a price at least one-sixteenth above that inside bid. The NASD's bid test rule was subject to enumerated exemptions. This type of regulation, limiting the price at which a short sale may be entered is generally referred to as a "tick test."

1934 Act Rule 10a–2 addressed collateral short sales. In short, the rule is designed to assure that a short sale is covered only when the customer has purchased the security or has properly borrowed the security for delivery for sale. Uncovered, or "naked," short sales are manipulative and hence in violation of the 1934 Act.

Short sales are now governed by Regulation SHO, which replaced 1934 Act Rules 10a–1 and 10b–2, incorporating their terms into the more comprehensive short sale regulations. Regulation SHO provides a quite complex and technical regulation of short sales. Regulation SHO also included a temporary rule embodying a pilot program which established procedures for the SEC to temporarily suspend operation of the "tick" test, as well as any short sale price test of any exchange or FINRA. Following the pilot program, the SEC abandoned the tick test for short sales, when it eliminated the tick test rule in July 2007. In the spring of 2009, the SEC proposed two alternative approaches to regulating short sales. The SEC presented two proposals, each with an alternative version. The first proposal was to implement a "short sale price test" or "short sale price test restriction" that would take the place of the former uptick rule. The second proposal was to implement a circuit breaker rule that would be triggered by a significant price decline in a particular security and would either halt short selling in that security or, under the alternative proposal would trigger a short sale price test. See Sec. Exch. Act Rel. No. 34–59748 (SEC April 10, 2009). In 2010, the SEC adopted what was known as the "alternative uptick circuit-breaker rule." See Amendments to Regulation SHO, Sec. Exch. Act Rel. No. 34–61595, 2010 WL 675942 (SEC Feb. 26, 2010).The rule as adopted rejected a permanent uptick rule and instead only applies when triggered by a ten percent decline sufficient to trigger the circuit breaker.

Regulation SHO provides further that short sellers of equity securities must locate securities to borrow before selling. In 2008, the SEC also adopted Rule 10b–21 that prohibits naked short selling by entering a short sale with the intent not to provide sufficient shares to effect delivery for the short sale. Rule 204 of Regulation SHO, adopted in 2009, sets forth broker-dealer obligations regarding pre-borrowing of securities for short sales and what to do in the case of a failure to deliver the securities for sale. Short selling prior to or in connection with a distribution can make it difficult for issuers to complete public offerings. Short sales in anticipation of a public offering do not involve the same market risks as short sales generally. See, e.g., Sec.Act Rel. No. 33–6798, Sec.Exch.Act Rel. No. 34–26028 (SEC Aug. 25, 1988). Since the pending offering will bring additional supply into the market, there will be downward price pressure. Such guaranteed downward price pressure is not ordinarily present in the securities markets. Limiting short sales during distributions necessarily has an adverse impact on short sellers. Notwithstanding the arguments to the contrary, the SEC concluded that this is justified in light of the potential for manipulation resulting from short sales in connection with public offerings.

As noted above, as a result of SEC rules, short selling prior to or in connection with a distribution can make it difficult for issuers to complete public offerings. Short sales in anticipation of a public offering do not involve the same market risks as short sales generally. Since the pending offering will bring additional supply into the market, there will be downward price pressure. Such guaranteed downward price pressure is not ordinarily present in the securities markets. Limiting short sales during distributions necessarily has an adverse impact on short sellers. Notwithstanding the arguments to the contrary, the Commission concluded that this is justified in light of the potential for manipulation resulting from short sales in connection with public offerings.

Under Rule 105 of SEC Reg. M, there is a period following the effective date during which short sales of securities made prior to the effective date may not be covered with securities issued in a cash offering that have been acquired from an underwriter or dealer participating in the public offering. The rule's prohibition applies to short sales made during the shorter of two periods: (a) the period beginning five days before the pricing of the offering and ending when the offering is priced or (b) the period beginning with the initial filing of the registration statement of Regulation A's Form 1–A and ending with the pricing of the offering. Securities issued pursuant to a shelf registration under 1933 Act Rule 415 are specifically excluded from Rule 105's purview.

Short sales during a tender offer can also have consequences under the securities laws. Thus, for example, in applying the prohibitions against the hedged tendering of securities in connection with a tender offer (1934 Act Rule 14e–4), a court may integrate a short sale of a security made around the time of the short seller's tendering of the securities to a tender offeror.

Investors can use derivative investments to take a short position. For example, purchasing a put option on a particular security gives the investor the right (before the option expires) to sell the security at the exercise price to the writer of the put option. If the price of the security declines below the option exercise price, then the option is "in the money" which means that if the option is exercised and the underlying security is then sold, the investor would realize a profit. There would cease to be a profit once the price of the stock climbs above the option exercise price since the investor could purchase the security more cheaply on the open market than by exercising his or her put option.

When an investor writes (or sells) a put option, the investor takes a "short" investment position and therefore involves similar risks as short sales and sales against the box. However, the writing of put options is not expressly covered by the short sale regulations discussed below.

Trading in puts and calls may result in an investment position similar to a short sale. However, these derivative positions do not necessarily implicate the short sale provisions. In fact, the SEC has been willing to grant no action relief from the short sale provisions with respect to certain derivative investment products. *See, e.g.,* Pharmaceutical Boxes, 2001 WL 1803376 (SEC No Action Letter Nov. 9, 2001).

§ 71. Parking

A practice that is clearly deceptive and may be manipulative is known as "parking." Parking occurs when an investor or broker transfers his or her securities to a third party for the purpose of hiding the true ownership. The SEC has described parking as "the sale of securities subject to an agreement or understanding that the securities will be repurchased by the seller at a later time and at a price which leaves the economic risk on the seller." In re Barlage, 63 S.E.C. 1060, 1996 WL 733756 at *1 n. 2 (SEC 1996). When this type of transfer occurs, it clearly qualifies as deceptive within the meaning of 1934 Act § 10(b). Parking is a sham transaction and thus, in addition to constituting deceptive conduct, is also properly characterized as manipulation.

Usually, the critical issue in a parking case is establishing whether the arrangements relating to the transactions in question involve bona fide purchases and sales, or, instead, are sham transactions designed to conceal true ownership. There are five factors to be considered in determining whether parking has taken place. The first factor is whether the trades were settled in the ordinary course of business or whether they were cancelled before settlement. Second, the existence of restrictions on resales may invite unscrupulous participants to engage in a parking scheme. Third, if the ostensible buyer does not bear any risk of loss, then parking may be involved. A fourth factor is whether the sales were transacted at the market price. Finally, in a parking transaction, typically the transaction does not take place at arm's length.

Parking can arise in various contexts. Broker-dealers have engaged in illegal parking in order to avoid the impact of the SEC's net capital rules. By temporarily selling securities from the brokerage firm's account to a customer's account in exchange for cash, the firm is able to avoid a discount (or "haircut") that otherwise would be applied against the value of the securities for the purpose of determining whether the firm is in compliance with the net capital requirements. After the report is filed, the firm then transfers the cash (plus interest) back to the customer's account in exchange for the securities that have been parked there to evade the net capital requirement. In contrast, a transaction entered into for the purpose of shifting the haircut from one account to another is not improper, since there is merely a shifting of the discount rather than an evasion.

Parking also occurs when broker-dealers park stock in order to withdraw it from the market, thereby restricting the supply available with the goal of artificially manipulating the price upwards.

A variation of parking is to transfer securities to "nominees" for the purpose of hiding the illusory nature of a manipulative transaction or series of transactions. Nominees have also been used in order to try to disguise "free riding" schemes, whereby securities are purchased without any intent to pay for the securities except out of profits from their subsequent sale.

Not every sale followed by a repurchase between accounts will constitute parking. Bona fide transactions that carry a true shift in investment risk following the initial sale are not improper parking transactions.

§ 72.   Broker–Dealer Bankruptcy—The Securities Investor Protection Act

During the 1960s, a large number of brokerage firms experienced various types of severe financial problems, including insolvency. Many investors allow their securities to be held by their brokers so that the brokers are the registered owners of the securities. This is often referred to as holding the securities in "street name." When customers' securities are held in street name, the broker's insolvency creates a substantial risk of harm in addition to that resulting from the broker-dealer's inability to honor or follow through with customer orders. Congress responded to these risks with the Securities Investor Protection Act of 1970 (SIPA). The Act established the Securities Investor Protection Corporation (SIPC), a nonprofit corporation whose membership is made up of most broker-dealers registered under the 1934 Act.

SIPC, which operates under SEC supervision, has two primary functions. First, SIPC is responsible for establishing and maintaining a fund for the benefit of injured investors. In this regard, SIPC is similar in nature to the Federal Deposit Insurance Corporation (FDIC), which protects depositors in commercial banks, and formerly the Federal Savings and Loan Insurance Corporation (FSLIC), the counterpart for depositors in savings and loan associations. Second, the SIPC becomes a party to proceedings to liquidate insolvent brokerage firms, which are conducted in a manner similar to that provided under the federal bankruptcy laws, including the appointment of a trustee. Unlike the federal bankruptcy laws, however, there is no provision under the SIPA for reorganization as an alternative to liquidation. SIPC may bring suit against third parties on behalf of the customers of the insolvent brokerage firm. SIPC's standing to bring suit exists notwithstanding the statute's failure to expressly list the authority to sue because bringing a suit for damages falls within SIPC's authority to pursue the insolvent brokerage firm's revenue in the ordinary course of business.

The SIPC fund is maintained by both initial and periodic assessment of the members. The fund is available to provide cash advances to injured customers who have valid claims against the insolvent broker-dealer in the liquidation proceedings. Any such advance is limited to five hundred thousand dollars per customer, but is not to exceed one hundred thousand dollars if the customer has a claim only for cash as opposed to a claim for securities. SIPC may also, in its discretion, advance to the trustee for the liquidation proceedings funds (1) to pay or guarantee indebtedness to a bank or other lender, (2) to secure indemnification of SIPC members against cash shortages, and (3) to purchase securities for the satisfaction of customer claims against the insolvent broker-dealers.

The protection of SIPA is generally reserved for customers of broker-dealers. Not every transaction effected through a securities broker and involving securities will classify someone delivering securities to a broker-dealer as a customer with regard to the transaction in question. In general, the courts have avoided interpreting the concept of customer too expansively. A successful SIPC claimant must demonstrate that he or she in fact had funds or securities on deposit with a broker-dealer. Further, in order to present a claim under the Securities Investor Protection Act, the customer must have had either a cash balance or an equity balance at the time of the brokerage firm's bankruptcy filing date. Customers' claims have different rights depending upon whether they are net equity claims based upon cash or securities. Not every customer's grievance against the broker-dealer will result in a SIPA claim. Even where customers are able to assert a claim, it has been held that there is no direct right of action against SIPC.

Beyond its ability to provide for cash advances to claimant customers and to advance funds to the trustee in liquidation, SIPC can, under appropriate circumstances, make direct payments in lieu of instituting liquidation proceedings. The direct payment procedure can be instituted only when the claims of all customers are less than two hundred and fifty thousand dollars in the aggregate. The direct payment procedure under SIPA is commenced by giving notice to all customers and publishing such notice in an appropriate newspaper. Anyone who feels aggrieved by a direct payment program has six months to file a claim in any court that would have jurisdiction under the federal bankruptcy laws. Although the direct payment procedure is of somewhat limited value due to the limitation on aggregate claims, it does provide a procedure that is much more expeditious than a full-fledged court-supervised liquidation. The more common liquidation proceedings, which are subject to the special role of the SIPC as described above, are conducted in conformance with the general procedures of the federal bankruptcy laws. Consideration of the bankruptcy laws is beyond the scope of this text and other sources should be consulted.

SIPA § 14(b) empowers the SEC to bar or suspend brokerage firm principals from associating with brokers and dealers. This is in addition to the comparable power given to the SEC under the 1934 Act.

CHAPTER 6

CIVIL LIABILITIES

§ 73. Applicability of Antifraud and Anti-manipulation Provisions

As discussed earlier, the 1934 Act's generalized antifraud Rule 10b–5 supports an implied private right of action permitting injured investors to sue for damages (§ 18 supra). 1934 Act § 9(e) provides a private remedy for manipulations taking place on an exchange. Manipulations on an exchange or in the NASDAQ and OTC markets are often in violation of 1934 Act Rule 10b–5. The courts have been reluctant to imply additional remedies, although there is sparse authority that some may exist.

§ 74. Private Remedies Against Exchanges, FINRA, and the NASD for Damages Resulting From Non-enforcement of Their Own Rules

On occasion, a self-regulatory organization will fail to enforce its own rules. In such situations, can the self-regulatory organization be held accountable for losses resulting from the failure to enforce its rules? The case law under the 1934 Act is relatively sparse, although there is some authority for the existence of a private remedy in appropriate cases to redress non-enforcement of securities exchanges' customer protection rules. Analogies can be made to the more substantial body of law that recognized a private remedy against commodity exchanges for enforcement lapses. The federal regulatory patterns which govern the securities and commodities industries have obvious parallels. It follows that the decisions recognizing a right of action under the Commodity Exchange Act may add support to the existence of a comparable remedy under the Exchange Act.

a. *Actions Against Securities Exchanges*

The courts have been in conflict as to the existence of an implied remedy against exchanges under the 1934 Act. In a relatively early decision in Baird v. Franklin, 141 F.2d 238 (2d Cir. 1944), cert. denied 323 U.S. 737 (1944), the Second Circuit, utilizing a "tort theory" of statutory implication, recognized a remedy against a securities exchange for failure to enforce its rules. A successful claim would depend upon a showing that the exchange acted in bad faith in failing to enforce its rules. The purported basis for the implied remedy against exchanges has been 1934 Act § 6, which requires the registration of national securities exchanges in accordance with SEC oversight. This "tort theory" of an implied right of action under 1934 Act § 6 has been followed by other federal courts that have recognized the remedy against a securities exchange. Although a similar tort rationale was subsequently used by the Supreme Court to recognize an implied remedy under the proxy rules (J.I. Case Co.

v. Borak, 377 U.S. 426 (1964)), this basis for implying federal rights of action has since been discred-
ited by more recent Supreme Court decisions. E.g.,
Cort v. Ash, 422 U.S. 66 (1975).

More in line with the restrictive approach to
additional implied rights of action generally, the
Third Circuit in Walck v. American Stock Exchange, Inc., 687 F.2d 778 (3d Cir. 1982), cert.
denied 461 U.S. 942 (1983), denied the existence of
an implied right of action against a securities exchange. The Third Circuit, applying the Supreme
Court's four-factor test from *Cort v. Ash*, found that
the 1934 Act was devoid of any indication of a
legislative intent to create such a right of action
against a securities exchange.

b.   *Actions Against the NASD and FINRA*

The cases discussed above deal with private suits
against securities exchanges, but what about the
other self-regulatory organization-namely, the
NASD and now FINRA? It is clear that a mere
negligent failure to supervise its members will not
support a private suit against the NASD. FDIC v.
National Association of Securities Dealers, 747 F.2d
498 (8th Cir. 1984). It has also been held that an
action will not lie against the NASD for an alleged
wrongful refusal to enforce its own rules. Aside
from the presence or absence of a private right of
action, as is the case with the exchanges, the NASD
enjoys immunity with regard to challenges to the
exercise of its oversight responsibility. Sparta Surgi-
cal Corp. v. NASD, 159 F.3d 1209 (9th Cir. 1998).

A broker challenging sanctions imposed by the NASD's Regional Business Conduct Committee must first exhaust his or her administrative remedies (such as an appeal to the NASD) before challenging the action in court. Marchiano v. NASD, 134 F.Supp.2d 90 (D.D.C. 2001). The federal court of appeals is the appropriate forum for judicial review of NASD disciplinary proceedings.

c. *Private Rights of Action for Nonenforcement of Rules by the Commodities Markets*

Prior to 1982, there was a substantial body of law under the Commodity Exchange Act (CEA) recognizing an implied right of action against commodities exchanges and their employees for a bad faith refusal to comply with their enforcement obligations. In 1982, the United States Supreme Court accepted this line of cases. Merrill Lynch, Pierce, Fenner & Smith v. Curran, 456 U.S. 353 (1982). Congress responded by replacing the implied remedy with an express right of action. CEA § 22.

In recognizing the implied right of action, the Supreme Court noted that although it was not as well-ingrained as the implied remedy under 1934 Act Rule 10b–5, there was a well-established line of cases recognizing the remedy. The Court observed that by the time the CEA was amended in 1974, Congress was fully aware that the courts had been implying private rights of action under the Act and thus Congress could be viewed as acquiescing in this line of cases. The Court was sharply divided in *Merrill Lynch, Pierce, Fenner & Smith v. Curran*, with four of the justices viewing the legislative history as not supporting an implied remedy. The implied remedy recognized by the Court imposed a higher standard of culpability than the familiar scienter requirement. Actions against exchanges, contract markets, registered futures associations, or their officials expressly require a showing that the defendant acted in bad faith. The bad faith requirement has been equated with a showing of an "ulterior motive." The bad faith requirement thus focuses on the intent behind the action, not upon its effects.

What do these developments under the CEA tell us about the securities law issues? First, the policies underlying the commodities and securities laws are sufficiently similar to warrant a strong analogy, at least with regard to the efficacy of implying a private remedy to redress SRO enforcement lapses. Second, the intent of Congress in instituting extensive market regulatory programs under both statutes would also seem to be similar. On the other hand, in 1982 Congress elected to replace the implied remedy under the CEA with an express remedy that finds no counterpart under the securities laws. Arguably, the absence of a parallel provision limiting implied remedies under the federal securities laws evidences a Congressional intent to allow implied private rights of action against securities exchanges, FINRA, or the NASD.

§ 75. Private Remedies Against Market Professionals

As discussed earlier, 1934 Act §§ 15 and 19 impose a self regulatory structure for broker-dealer regulation under the auspices of FINRA (formerly the NASD) and the national securities exchanges. Many of the applicable regulations are properly classified as customer protection rules. While violations of the applicable regulatory provisions can result in disciplinary sanction by the SEC, NASD (FINRA), or exchange, there is substantial authority against the recognition of an implied right of action in the hands of injured investors against the violator.

a.   *1934 Act § 15(c)*

1934 Act § 15(c)(1) makes it unlawful for a broker or dealer "to effect any transaction in, or to induce or attempt to induce the purchase or sale of any security * * * by means of any manipulative, deceptive or other fraudulent device." On its face, § 15(c) appears to contain the requirement that the conduct be deceptive or manipulative, as is the case with 1934 Act § 10(b). Accordingly, it would appear that negligent conduct cannot provide the basis for a § 15 violation.

Although there has been considerable case law, the courts are divided as to whether a private right of action is to be implied under 1934 Act § 15(c). Compare, e.g., Speck v. Oppenheimer & Co., 583 F.Supp. 325 (W.D.Mo. 1984) (customer had implied right of action to redress broker-dealer's fraud) with Goodman v. Shearson Lehman Brothers, Inc., 698 F.Supp. 1078 (S.D.N.Y. 1988) (holding there is no implied right of action under section 15). While the older cases tended to recognize an implied remedy under 1934 Act § 15(c), the trend in the more recent cases is not to recognize the remedy. This is far from surprising in light of the decline of implied remedies in general.

b. FINRA, NASD, and Exchange Rules

As for violations of exchange or NASD rules, it was generally held that violation of a rule of a self-regulatory organization will not, by itself, support a private right of action. Spicer v. Chicago Board Options Exchange, Inc., 977 F.2d 255 (7th Cir. 1992); Craighead v. E.F. Hutton & Co., 899 F.2d 485 (6th Cir. 1990). The result would be the same with respect to FINRA rules. However, a violation of an exchange, FINRA, or NASD rule can form the basis of a 1934 Act Rule 10b–5 action, provided, of course, that all of the elements of a 10b–5 claim can be established. (See § 18 supra). Thus, for example, it is well established that a broker-dealer who churns a customer's account can be held accountable for damages under 1934 Act Rule 10b–5. (See § 68 supra).

c. 1934 Act Rule 10b–5

Various brokerage practices have been held actionable under 1934 Act Rule 10b–5. See § 18 supra. Thus, for example, a brokerage firm's alleged policy of clearing customers' funds through remotely located banks in order to earn more interest on the funds was held to support an action under Rule 10b–5. Ellis v. Merrill Lynch & Co., 664 F.Supp. 979 (E.D.Pa. 1987). In contrast, however, an alleged scheme to delay customer payments of dividends was held not to be in violation of Rule 10b–5 since it was not in connection with the purchase or sale of a security. Id.

The Supreme Court gave an expansive definition of what constitutes fraud *in connection with* the purchase or sale of a security. In SEC v. Zandford, 535 U.S. 813 (2002), the SEC brought suit against a stock broker who emptied his client's account and converted the proceeds. The Second Circuit held there was no fraud in connection with specific securities transactions; therefore, 1934 Act Rule 10b–5 should not be used to challenge the broker's actions. The Supreme Court reversed, reasoning that the purpose of the federal securities laws was to assure the existence of honest securities markets and to promote investor confidence. There was deception insofar as the broker failed to disclose to his customer the challenged embezzlement out of a securities account and that this was sufficient connection to establish securities fraud.

Although most courts do not recognize a private right of action for a violation of the margin requirements, material misrepresentations in connection with margin transactions may result in liability under 1934 Act Rule 10b–5. Some courts have recognized an implied right of action under 1934 Act Rule 10b–16, which mandates full disclosure in connection with credit transactions.

Failure to comply with 1934 Act Rule 10b–10's disclosure requirements relating to sales confirmations can also result in liability via the implied remedy under 1934 Act Rule 10b–5. Thus, for example, nondisclosure of market maker status can be actionable under 1934 Act Rule 10b–5. Furthermore, compliance with 1934 Act Rule 10b–10 does not preclude an action under Rule 10b–5 for misrepresentations in connection with securities transactions.

A broker's misrepresentations concerning the amount of commissions being charged clearly is actionable. Hoxworth v. Blinder, Robinson & Co., 903 F.2d 186 (3d Cir. 1990). However, to be actionable, the misstatements must have been material and the customer must have relied on them. Thus, excessive mark-ups that give a materially misleading impression of the actual market price are fraudulent. The foregoing represent examples of the types of broker-dealer conduct and representations that under appropriate facts may be held actionable as fraud.

d. 1933 Act Liability

Misconduct by broker-dealers can also result in liability under the 1933 Act. When a broker-dealer makes material misrepresentations in connection with a customer's purchase of a security, liability can also result under 1933 ACT § 12(a)(2). Unlike 1934 Act Rule 10b–5, 1933 ACT § 12(a)(2) does not have a scienter requirement. However, 1933 ACT § 12(a)(2) is limited in scope as it applies only to misstatements made in connection with a public offering. Gustafson v. Alloyd Co., 513 U.S. 561 (1995).

Broker-dealers who act as underwriters in 1933 Act registered offerings will be liable under 1933 Act § 11 for material misstatements and omissions in the registration materials unless they can sustain the burden of proving their due diligence defense. The due diligence defense requires a showing that the underwriter made an independent investigation before signing off on the registration statement.

A broker-dealer who sells a security in violation of the 1933 Act § 5's registration requirements will be liable in an action for rescission under 1933 Act § 12(a)(1).

e. *IAA Liability*

Broker-dealers who render investment advice incidental to their broker-dealer operations need not register as investment advisers under the IAA. Similarly, since such broker-dealers are excluded from the definition of investment adviser, they are not subject to IAA § 206's antifraud section provisions. However, broker-dealers whose investment adviser functions are more than incidental to their brokerage services and therefore subject to the additional regulation of the 1940 IAA are also subject to § 206.

§ 76. Secondary Liability of Broker–Dealer Firms

Of particular interest in broker-dealer litigation is the extent to which the brokerage firm can be held accountable for actionable violations by its account executives or other employees. The three principal vehicles for imposing such liability are: (1) statutorily created controlling person liability, (2) for the brokerage firm's culpable failure to supervise its employees, and (3) under common law principles of vicarious liability of employers generally.

a.   *Controlling Person Liability*

1934 Act § 20(a) states that "[e]very person who, directly or indirectly, controls any person liable under any provision of this chapter or of any rule or regulation thereunder shall also be liable jointly and severally with and to the same extent as such controlled person * * *." Thus, for a controlling person to be liable, the person over who control was exercised must have committed a primary violation of the securities laws. Otherwise, the controlled person will not be held accountable and subsequently, the controlling person will have no liability in which to share jointly and severally. 1934 Act § 20(a) of the Exchange Act closely parallels 1933 Act § 15 of the 1933 Act, except that the 1933 Act provision is limited to actions under § 11 or § 12 of that Act. 1934 Act § 20(a) is not expressly limited and thus applies to both express and implied remedies under the Exchange Act.

1934 Act § 20(a) controlling person liability requires not only that the defendant be a control person of the primary violator, but also that the defendant was a culpable participant in the illegal activity. Controlling person liability will not apply when the controlling person acted in good faith and was not aware of the primary violator's activities. When dealing with broker-dealers, the courts have employed a more relaxed test to determine if there is sufficient culpability to invoke controlling person liability for the acts of their employees. Failure to supervise a broker-dealer is deemed to be indirect participation by the controlling person, and thus the controlling person may be liable under 1934 Act § 20(a) for any fraudulent schemes arising during the unsupervised period. See, e.g., Harrison v. Dean Witter Reynolds, Inc., 79 F.3d 609 (7th Cir. 1996).

Controlling person liability is limited to transactions taking place on behalf of the employer or other controlling person. Thus, for example, when a customer is dealing with a sales representative in his or her private capacity without relying on any affiliation with the employer brokerage firm, the firm will not be held accountable as a controlling person. On the other hand, when an employee is acting under the firm's auspices, controlling person liability and control depends upon control over the broker generally; control with regard to the particular transaction in question need not be shown. Martin v. Shearson Lehman Hutton, 986 F.2d 242 (8th Cir. 1993). Controlling person liability is based on the possession of the power to control the primary violator and thus does not depend on the actual exercise of that power. See, e.g., IBS Financial Corp. v. Seidman & Associates, 136 F.3d 940 (3d Cir. 1998).

Controlling person liability requires more than a tangential connection to the conduct in question.

Thus, for example, even where the brokerage customer had a bank account with a parent of the brokerage firm, the parent/subsidiary relationship was not sufficient to hold the parent bank liable for the brokerage firm's alleged wrongdoing. Abbell Credit Corp. v. Bank of America Corp., 2002 WL 335320 (N.D.Ill. 2002).

b. *Respondeat Superior*

Various common law theories have been used to hold brokerage firms accountable for their employees' violations. A principal may be held liable under common law if the principal actually authorizes the tort committed by his agent. Liability may also be based on the "apparent authority" of the agent. Under this theory, a principal may be liable for the torts of its agents if the agents act under the guise of apparent authority from the corporation.

There is a division of authority whether the statutory imposition of controlling person liability was intended to displace common law agency principles. A number of circuit courts have held that 1934 Act § 20(a) is not an exclusive remedy. It follows that common law principles of respondeat superior may also be applied.

Controlling person liability is more restrictive than common law agency theories in that it holds a controlling person liable only if that person (1) did not act in good faith or (2) induced or knowingly participated in the violation. On the other hand, "common law agency theories may impose liability on a principal or employer without these two 'preconditions.' " In re Atlantic Financial Management, Inc., 784 F.2d 29, 30 (1st Cir. 1986).

c. *Failure to Supervise*

In addition to the duty to supervise that may exist under agency principles, the securities laws and SRO rules impose upon broker-dealers a duty to supervise their employees. See § 27 supra. This duty provides the basis for administrative sanctions and does not extend expressly to private litigation. However, a failure to supervise can be the basis of controlling person liability.

d. *Aiding and Abetting Liability*

Brokers are frequently brought into securities law claims against other defendants based on the charge that the broker-dealer aided and abetted the primary violation. Aiding and abetting liability requires a showing of "(1) the existence of a securities law violation by the primary party * * * (2) 'knowledge' of the violation on the part of the aider and abettor, and (3) 'substantial assistance' by the aider and abettor in the achievement of the primary violation." Metge v. Baehler, 762 F.2d 621 (8th Cir. 1985), cert. denied 474 U.S. 1057 (1986).

In Central Bank of Denver v. First Interstate Bank of Denver, 511 U.S. 164 (1994), the Supreme Court held in a five-to-four decision that there is no implied right of action to redress aiding and abetting a 1934 Act Rule 10b–5 violation. That decision, however, does not have an impact on broker-dealer litigation involving the SEC or on the criminal prosecution since there is express statutory authority for pursuing broker-dealers as aiders and abettors (1934 Act § 15(b)(4)). However, private litigants are precluded by the *Central Bank* case from pursuing brokers and their firms as aiders and abettors.

Following the *Central Bank* decision, a key question in private litigation is whether the defendant was a primary violator rather than merely an aider and abettor. The line between primary and secondary is not always easily drawn. Some courts have held that in order to be a primary violator the defendant must have drafted or uttered the statements forming the basis of the fraud suit. Other courts held that primary liability could be found if the defendant knowingly participated in the fraudulent scheme even though he or she was not responsible for the statements at issue. The Supreme Court's decision in Stoneridge Investment Partners, LLC v. Scientific–Atlanta, Inc., 552 U.S. 148 (2008) likely put an end to this so-called scheme liability, at least in private suits. Among other things, the Court held that the defendant's involvement in the misrepresentations in question must have been apparent to the plaintiff so as to satisfy the reliance requirement in private actions under Rule 10b–5.

CHAPTER 7

ARBITRATION OF BROKER–DEALER DISPUTES

§ 77. Enforcement of Broker–Dealer Arbitration Agreements

At one time, pre-dispute arbitration agreements were unenforceable with regard to claims arising under the federal securities laws. This meant that virtually all claims by customers against their securities brokers were resolved in court or by settlement. In Wilko v. Swan, 346 U.S. 427 (1953), the Supreme Court held that a court could not compel arbitration of claims asserted under 1933 Act § 12(a)(2) despite the existence of an arbitration agreement between the plaintiff and the defendant broker. The court relied on the language of 1933 Act § 14, which states that: "Any condition, stipulation or provision binding any person acquiring any security to waive compliance with any provision of this subchapter or of the rules and regulations of the Commission shall be void." Since Congress specifically granted persons asserting federal securities claims the right to bring suit in federal court, the Court decided that the intention of Congress would be best effectuated by invalidating arbitration agreements with respect to Securities Act claims. Following *Wilko*, courts at first were consistent in holding that agreements to arbitrate claims arising under the 1934 Act were equally invalid because the 1934 Act § 29(a) contains an anti-waiver provision almost identical to the one found in 1933 Act § 14.

The *Wilko* doctrine eroded over time. The Supreme Court overruled *Wilko* and held that pre-dispute arbitration agreements between brokers and their customers are enforceable. Rodriguez de Quijas v. Shearson/American Express, 490 U.S. 477 (1989); Shearson/American Express, Inc. v. McMahon, 482 U.S. 220 (1987). Not surprisingly, most brokerage firms routinely require customers to sign pre-dispute arbitration agreements. Accordingly, most disputes between customers and their brokers now are decided in arbitral forums rather than in court. One consequence of this shift has been that much of the law relating to broker-dealer litigation has been placed in a state of suspended animation as it existed in the pre-arbitration era. This is the case because relatively few private disputes will continue to be litigated in court and there is a narrow standard for judicial review of arbitrators' decisions.

Arbitration is not limited to customer disputes but is also used for resolution of disputes within the brokerage industry. In fact, the Form U–4 that is used by FINRA and most states requires arbitration of member disputes.

The demise of the *Wilko* doctrine has not eliminated questions relating to the parties' ability to select an arbitral forum for the resolution of disputes arising under the federal securities laws.

Thus, depending on the terms of the arbitration clause, disputes can still exist as to which is the appropriate arbitral forum.

§ 78. No Arbitration for Class Actions

Many actions for securities fraud arise in the context of a class action. On occasion, a class action may be appropriate for customer disputes with broker-dealers. With the overruling of the *Wilko* doctrine, questions arose regarding the arbitrability of customer/broker disputes that were brought as class actions. The three major arbitral forums (NASD, NYSE, and AMEX) adopted rules that precluded the bringing of class actions, thus requiring class action plaintiffs to go to court unless, for arbitration agreements effective prior to 1993, a different arbitral forum has been selected. FINRA retains the rule against class actions in arbitration.

Many of the procedural provisions necessary to resolve complex class actions are not available in the SRO arbitration programs. Exch. Act Rel. No. 34–31371, 57 Fed Reg. 52659, at 52661 (Nov. 4, 1992). Thus, class actions are better handled in the courts.

§ 79. The Federal Arbitration Act

As the preceding cases demonstrate, the Federal Arbitration Act (FAA) (9 U.S.C.A. §§ 1) embodies a strong public policy favoring arbitration. There are limits, however, to the FAA's impact. Thus, for example, the FAA does not create a basis for federal jurisdiction independent of that which might be available under the federal securities laws. Baltin v.

Alaron Trading Corp., 128 F.3d 1466 (11th Cir. 1997) (Federal Arbitration Act does not create federal jurisdiction over state law claims); Prudential–Bache Securities, Inc. v. Fitch, 966 F.2d 981 (5th Cir. 1992). Similarly, although the FAA applies to claims involving interstate commerce, it does not apply to a transaction that is wholly intrastate. Ex parte Jones, 628 So.2d 316 (Ala. 1993). On the other hand, when the jurisdictional reach of the Federal Arbitration Act is implicated, that act may preempt the applicable state law. Olde Discount Corp. v. Tupman, 1 F.3d 202 (3d Cir. 1993) (Federal Arbitration Act may preclude state action seeking rescission pending outcome of arbitration).

In Mastrobuono v. Shearson Lehman Hutton, Inc., 514 U.S. 52 (1995), the Court ruled that a state procedural rule barring punitive damages in arbitration proceedings must yield to the procedural rules of the FAA in light of the broad policy favoring arbitration under that Act. The Court held that the parties' choice of law clause meant that the state's substantive law permitting punitive damages applied but not the procedural bar. See also, e.g., Doctor's Associates, Inc. v. Casarotto, 517 U.S. 681 (1996) (FAA preempts Montana statute which conditioned enforceability of arbitration clause on compliance with special notice requirements); Perry v. Thomas, 482 U.S. 483 (1987) (FAA preempts California labor law exempting certain employment claims from pre-existing arbitration clauses).

Another example of the policy favoring arbitration is found in the Second Circuit's ruling that a customer can demand arbitration, notwithstanding the fact that the broker and customer had mutually agreed to cross out the arbitration clause contained in the customer agreement. Kidder, Peabody & Co. v. Zinsmeyer Trusts Partnership, 41 F.3d 861 (2d Cir. 1994). The court so ruled in light of the broker-dealer's preexisting duty to arbitrate under the NASD's Arbitration Code. The net effect of this ruling is to give the customer an option to arbitrate even in instances where the brokerage firm does not have the ability to compel arbitration.

Notwithstanding the strong policies of the Arbitration Act, policy considerations may have to yield to the express language of the securities laws. Thus, a three judge panel of the Ninth Circuit refused to enforce an arbitration clause for arbitration outside the United States where there were substantial contacts in the United States and enforcement of the arbitration clause would have resulted in a foreign country's law being applied. Richards v. Lloyd's of London, 107 F.3d 1422 (9th Cir. 1997). The court reasoned that this would amount to an impermissible waiver of rights under the 1933 and 1934 Acts. However, in an en banc ruling the court held that there were sufficient contacts with England to uphold the choice of forum clause. Richards v. Lloyd's of London, 135 F.3d 1289 (9th Cir. 1998) (en banc).

§ 80. State Laws Affecting Arbitration Clauses

As noted above, the FAA plays a prominent role in determining arbitration issues in federal court.

But what about the role of state law? Massachusetts announced that effective January, 1989, broker-dealers doing business in that state must offer customers the option of not signing pre-dispute arbitration agreements; however, that rule has since been struck down by a federal district court. Similar rules requiring that customers be given a choice were endorsed by the North American Securities Administrators Association and have been under consideration in at least sixteen additional states. Rather than invalidating all pre-dispute agreements, the Massachusetts rule provided that upon opening an account, customers must be given the option of not signing the arbitration clause. While an across-the-board ban on arbitration agreements might arguably be preempted by the federal policy favoring arbitration of securities disputes, mandating that customers be given a choice should be viewed as a valid exercise of state regulation.

Notwithstanding the argument that giving customers a choice does not conflict with federal policy, the First Circuit Court of Appeals invalidated the Massachusetts arbitration rules. Securities Industry Association v. Connolly, 883 F.2d 1114 (1st Cir. 1989), cert. denied 495 U.S. 956 (1990). Florida legislation provided that in any arbitration clause, customers must be given a choice of a non-industry arbitration forum. West's Fla.Stat.Ann. § 517.22. The Florida legislation was struck down. Securities Industry Association v. Lewis, 751 F.Supp. 205 (S.D.Fla. 1990). However, when the transaction in question is wholly intrastate, a valid state law invalidating pre-dispute arbitration will control. Ex parte Jones, 628 So.2d 316 (Ala. 1993).

In 2001 California Code of Civil Procedure was revised to require that within ten days of the proposed appointment of a neutral arbitrator, the neutral arbitrator disclose in writing "all matters that could cause a person aware of the facts to reasonably entertain a doubt that the proposed neutral arbitrator would be able to be impartial, including * * * [a]ny matters required to be disclosed by the ethics standards for neutral arbitrators adopted by the Judicial Council pursuant to this chapter." Cal. Code Civ. P. § 1281.9(a). Under the California statute, failure to provide the required disclosures creates grounds for disqualification of the neutral arbitrator. Further, the statute requires courts to vacate an arbitration award if an arbitrator fails to make timely disclosure of a ground for disqualification of which the arbitrator was then aware, or if the arbitrator was subject to disqualification but failed to disqualify himself or herself after being asked to do so by a party. The NASD and NYSE challenged the California rules on the basis that they are preempted by the federal securities laws with respect to securities arbitrations and the SEC supported their position. Although the initial challenge was dismissed, the courts eventually invalidated the California law. NASD Dispute Resolution, Inc. v. Judicial Council of State of Cal., 488 F.3d 1065 (9th Cir. 2007) (the district court's dismissal was rendered moot by federal and state decisions invalidating the California law). It is thus clear that state law cannot be used to unduly undercut the strong federal policy favoring arbitration as embodied in the FAA.

§ 81. Factors Affecting Enforcement of Pre-dispute Arbitration Agreements

As discussed in the preceding sections, it is now clear that the policies of the FAA favoring arbitration outweigh any contrary indications in the 1933 or 1934 Act. The fact that a dispute is arbitrable does not mean that all pre-dispute arbitration clauses are enforceable. See, e.g., Taylor v. Investors Associates, Inc., 29 F.3d 211 (5th Cir. 1994) (arbitration agreement between customer and clearing broker could not be enforced by a non-signing introducing broker who was not even mentioned in the agreement). The absence of a federal bar to arbitration and even the federal policy favoring arbitration does not alter the fact that in order to be enforced, the agreement to arbitrate must be enforceable under applicable contract and other state law principles.

Accordingly, various common law doctrines may come into play in determining the enforceability of pre-dispute arbitration agreements. The attacks on arbitration agreements have been made both on the grounds that they constitute unenforceable adhesion contracts and, alternatively, that the agreement should be avoided because of fraud in the inducement.

FAA § 2 provides that arbitration agreements can be invalidated upon such grounds that exist at law or equity for the invalidity of any contract. Thus, a court cannot compel arbitration unless there is a valid contractual obligation. Brokerage customers frequently seek to avoid pre-dispute arbitration agreements by claiming that the arbitration clause is an invalid contract of adhesion. The determination of whether there is an adhesion contract is highly factual and is difficult to prove.

The contract issues will generally be determined under state law. However, SRO rules may also affect the validity of arbitration clauses. Accordingly, failure to comply with the FINRA (formerly the NASD and NYSE) disclosure obligations, including the requirement that any agreement containing an arbitration clause be specifically acknowledged by the customer, can result in the invalidity, and hence unenforceability, of the arbitration agreement. See Mueske v. Piper, Jaffray & Hopwood, Inc., 260 Mont. 207, 859 P.2d 444 (1993).

The essence of the adhesion contract claim is that the use of arbitration clauses is an industry-wide practice and that it is unfair to force them upon customers. However, the majority of courts have held that there is nothing inherently unfair about arbitration clauses and thus the clause does not place the customer in an unfair position. Arbitration clauses have been upheld even though appearing on the reverse side of the brokerage agreement.

Many pre-dispute arbitration clauses provide that the dispute shall be heard in accordance with the arbitration rules of one of the exchanges or the

NASD. The exchanges and the NASD have transferred their arbitration programs to FINRA. These rules, which were adopted with SEC oversight, set out the arbitration procedures and method of arbitrator selection. A few courts have invalidated such agreements on the grounds that the exchange's selection of the arbitrators made the proceedings presumptively biased. However, most courts have not agreed with this presumption of bias, and the rationale of the Supreme Court's decisions in *Rodriguez* and *McMahon* (see § 77 supra) seems to undercut the finding of bias.

§ 82. Which Law Controls?

When dealing with the enforceability of pre-dispute arbitration agreements, there is an unusual mix of state and federal law. In the first instance, as discussed in previous sections, the policy favoring arbitration as embodied in the FAA militates in favor of enforcing pre-dispute arbitration agreements. On the other hand, interpreting the terms of any agreement between customers and securities brokers generally will be a matter of state contract law rather than federal securities or arbitration law. Ordinarily, state contract law will control whether the parties have in fact agreed to submit the controversy to arbitration. PaineWebber, Inc. v. Bybyk, 81 F.3d 1193, 1198 (2d Cir. 1996) ("Arbitration 'is a matter of contract and a party cannot be required to submit to arbitration any dispute which he has not agreed so to submit.' ") (quoting AT & T Techs., Inc. v. Communications Workers of America, 475 U.S. 643, 648 (1986)); Coleman & Co. Securities, Inc. v. Giaquinto Family Trust, 2000 WL 1683450 (S.D.N.Y. 2000) ("In deciding whether the parties agreed to arbitrate a matter, the courts ordinarily apply state law principles governing the formation of contracts").

There is not only a question of the choice of law between state and federal law, but there may also be an issue as to which forum—the court or arbitration panel—is to decide the enforceability of pre-dispute arbitration agreements. As is discussed later in this section, when it has been alleged that a party was fraudulently induced to enter into the entire contract, that claim should be addressed by the arbitrator rather than by a federal court. Houlihan v. Offerman & Co., 31 F.3d 692 (8th Cir. 1994). However, when the claim of fraud relates only to the agreement to arbitrate, it is appropriate to stay arbitration pending judicial resolution of the fraud claim. C.B.S. Employees Federal Credit Union v. Donaldson, Lufkin & Jenrette Securities Corp., 912 F.2d 1563 (6th Cir. 1990). The same rule has been said to apply to claims of coercion and adhesion contracts. Namely, if the claim of coercion or adhesion contract relates to the entire contract, the issue is to be determined by the arbitrators.

FAA § 4 provides that, upon application to a court to enforce an arbitration clause, the court must order arbitration unless "the making of the arbitration agreement or the failure, neglect, or refusal to perform the same be in issue," in which case the court shall try the issue of whether there is a valid agreement to arbitrate or if whether in the face of an agreement to arbitrate, there has been a breach of that agreement. Based on a narrow reading of this passage, some cases have given the court a somewhat limited role in deciding whether to send the dispute to arbitration. See, e.g., First Options of Chicago, Inc. v. Kaplan, 514 U.S. 938 (1995). However, other decisions give a broader reading to the powers of a court. In the Matter of VMS Limited Partnership Securities Litigation, 26 F.3d 50 (7th Cir. 1994) (whether there is a valid arbitration agreement is a question for the court). These decisions, giving broader power to the court, reason that if there is a question about the scope of coverage of the arbitration clause, the "failure, neglect, or refusal to perform" must be decided, because there cannot be an actionable failure to perform if the contract created no duty to arbitrate the particular issue. PaineWebber v. Hartmann, 921 F.2d 507, 510–11 (3d Cir. 1990). The court's job is therefore to decide if, according to the terms of the contract, the matter in dispute falls within the substantive scope of a valid arbitration agreement. The presumption of arbitrability means that it is within the scope of permissible arbitration unless it may be said "with positive assurance" that it is not.

§ 83. Who Decides the Issue of Arbitrability?

According to many decisions, if the arbitrability of a claim depends upon the validity of the contract in question, then it must be determined by a court. E.g., Roney & Co. v. Kassab, 981 F.2d 894 (6th Cir.

246 ARBITRATION OF DISPUTES Ch. 7

1992) (issue of parties' intent and determination of
whether NYSE Rule 603 required arbitration was to
be determined by the court). However, some courts
have held that the arbitrator can decide arbitrability issues. As a general rule, when the challenge is to
the validity of the contract as a whole, and not
specifically to the arbitration clause alone, the matter is to be determined by the arbitrator and not by
a court. *See* Buckeye Check Cashing, Inc. v. Cardeg-
na, 546 U.S. 440 (2006) (a claim contesting of the
legality and enforceability of a payday loan is subject to the arbitration clause of the contract; revers-
ing a decision of the Florida Supreme Court, the
U.S. Supreme Court ruled that the validity of the
arbitration clause could be separated from the loan
contract). Notwithstanding the broad policy favoring arbitration, questions of whether the parties in
fact agreed to arbitration is a matter for the courts
unless the parties have demonstrated a clear intent
to the contrary. Howsam v. Dean Witter Reynolds,
Inc., 537 U.S. 79 (2002).

§ 84. When Are Arbitration Clauses in Bro-
kers' Customer Agreements Contracts
of Adhesion?

The fact that pre-dispute arbitration agreements
are enforceable under the federal securities laws
does not negate other doctrines that may be available to challenge such an agreement. To the extent
that a pre-dispute arbitration agreement represents
a contract of adhesion, it may be disregarded.

FAA § 2 states that agreements to resort to arbitration can be invalidated upon such grounds that exist at law or equity for the revocation of any contract. Thus, a court cannot compel arbitration unless, as a matter of the relevant state law, a valid arbitration agreement exists. In the context of disputes arising out of securities transactions, brokerage customers frequently seek to avoid arbitration clauses by claiming the contracts are unenforceable contracts of adhesion. The basis of the customers' claim typically is that the customer stands in an unequal bargaining position vis a vis their broker. Furthermore, it is argued that since the use of arbitration clauses is an industry-wide practice, customers must agree to such a clause in order to participate in the securities market. Numerous decisions have rejected the adhesion contract attack on arbitration clauses.

Courts have developed a two-pronged test to determine whether an adhesion contract exists and is of the variety that renders the arbitration clause unenforceable. First, the courts examine whether the contractual clause in question was outside the expectations of the parties. In the context of broker's customer agreements, however, most courts have held that the arbitration clauses are within the expectations of the parties and thus are not to be disregarded as contracts of adhesion. Second, the courts examine whether the provision is unduly oppressive, unconscionable, or against public policy. The overwhelming majority of courts have held that there is nothing inherently unfair about an arbitration clause, and that the clause does not place the customer in an inferior position. Absent a showing of specific unfairness or overreaching, most courts will reject the contract of adhesion theory.

§ 85.   Use of Rules of Contract Interpretation to Determine Arbitrability

The cases questioning the enforceability of contracts of adhesion do not provide the only basis for attacking pre-dispute arbitration agreements. Other contract doctrines may be used to determine whether there is a binding agreement to arbitrate disputes. Principles of contract interpretation may be used to aid a customer's claim that the dispute in question is not covered by a pre-dispute arbitration clause. For example, under the plain meaning rule, a contract that clearly shows an intent to exclude a federal securities claim from an arbitration clause will be interpreted accordingly.

The interpretation of the contract language is determined as a matter of state rather than federal law. As a matter of the general law of contract interpretation, when the interpretation of a contract is in doubt, courts frequently construe the terms contrary to the interests of the party which drafted the contract. It is likely that this maxim of contract interpretation will carry over to pre-dispute arbitration clauses in securities cases. Ordinarily, contract interpretation issues will be highly factual. In some instances, however, the agreement may be sufficiently clear to support an interpretation as a matter of law.

§ 86. Claims of Unenforceability Based on Alleged Bias of the Arbitration Program

Often related to the claim that the arbitration clause is an unenforceable contract of adhesion is the claim that the clause should not be enforced because of the bias of the arbitration program. Many of the arbitration clauses provided that disputes will be arbitrated by the NYSE, and on occasion customers have argued that the clause is unfair, because the NYSE will be biased in favor of its members. In a pre–*McMahon* decision, a California state court invalidated an arbitration clause that required disputes to be resolved by the NYSE based on the exchange's ability to select the arbitration panel and because the arbitration rules further provided that the NYSE Board of Governors Exchange could change the arbitration rules. Richards v. Merrill Lynch, Pierce, Fenner & Smith, Inc., 64 Cal.App.3d 899, 135 Cal.Rptr. 26 (1976). Another pre-*McMahon* California decision held that the NYSE arbitration program was presumptively biased and that arbitration clauses requiring disputes to be resolved by the NYSE were unconscionable. The continuing validity of these two decisions became questionable in light of changes in the arbitration rules and the subsequent case of Parr v. Superior Court, 139 Cal.App.3d 440, 188 Cal.Rptr. 801 (1983). In *Parr* the court held the presumed bias of the NYSE had been rebutted. The court's decision found it significant that the SEC had approved the exchange's arbitration procedures. In addition, the court pointed to several rules that rebutted the

Where the claim of fraudulent inducement relates to the entire contract rather than the arbitration clause in particular, the claim should be addressed by the arbitrator rather than by a federal court. However, in the face of a customer's claim that the customer's assent had been fraudulently procured with regard to a margin agreement and arbitration clause, it is appropriate to stay arbitration pending judicial resolution of the fraud claim, which will determine whether the dispute must be sent to arbitration.

In order to establish that the arbitration clause was fraudulently induced, the customer must be able to prove specific misrepresentations (or fraudulent concealment) relating to the arbitration clause. *E.g.*, Rosen v. Waldman, 1993 WL 403974 (S.D.N.Y. 1993).

More generalized fraudulent statements may establish fraud in the entire agreement, but such claims are to be heard in arbitration.

§ 88. Waiver

Another question that arises with respect to the arbitration of disputes is one of waiver. It is possible to waive an agreement to arbitrate. A court may find an implied waiver of the agreement to arbitrate where that waiver is said to arise from participation in a lawsuit in a manner inconsistent with exercising the right to arbitration. Hoxworth v. Blinder, Robinson & Co., 980 F.2d 912 (3d Cir. 1992) (active litigation for over a year including extensive pretrial discovery and lengthy memorandum opposing class certification operated as a waiver of arbitration agreement); Stone v. E.F. Hutton & Co., 898 F.2d 1542 (11th Cir. 1990) (delay of more than twenty months in requesting arbitration and participation in pretrial discovery operated as a waiver of the right to arbitrate); MidAmerica Federal Savings & Loan Ass'n v. Shearson/American Express, Inc., 886 F.2d 1249, 1256 (10th Cir. 1989) (broker engaged in extensive litigation and therefore was found to have waived right to arbitration). Not every instance of participation in a law suit will necessarily act as a waiver of the right to arbitrate. For example it has been held that participation in pretrial discovery has been held not to act as a waiver of the arbitration agreement. Walker v. J.C. Bradford & Co., 938 F.2d 575 (5th Cir. 1991). Similarly, participation in an arbitration does not in and of itself waive any objections to the proceedings, especially where the participation consists of motions objecting to continuation. Prudential Securities, Inc. v. Hornsby, 865 F.Supp. 447 (N.D.Ill. 1994).

A party asserting that the right to arbitrate has been waived has a "heavy" burden of proof. A showing of active participation in judicial litigation generally is sufficient to meet this burden and thus will establish a waiver. It has been held that a failure to take a timely appeal from denial of a motion to compel arbitration operated as a waiver of any right to arbitration that may have existed. Once it is determined that there is a valid arbitration agreement, the determination of whether there has been a waiver of the right to arbitrate is to be determined by the arbitrators rather than a court. This is a consequence of the more general rule, that once it has been established that there is a valid arbitration agreement, procedural issues are for the arbitrators.

§ 89. Res Judicata and Collateral Estoppel

The state and self-regulatory organization arbitration procedures tend to be very efficient and will generally proceed to judgment more rapidly than a federal court suit. Accordingly, a byproduct of the duplicative adjudication is the possibility that the state law arbitration determination may be given preclusive effect in federal court under the doctrine of collateral estoppel. Courts consider a number of factors in determining whether to give preclusive effect to non-judicial and state court decisions. It is generally held that a grant of exclusive federal jurisdiction does not preclude res judicata or collateral estoppel based on a state court adjudication. Given that res judicata and collateral estoppel apply to state law proceedings, the next question is whether to apply them to non-judicial determinations. In general, the federal district courts have a wide range of discretion in deciding whether to apply collateral estoppel. *E.g.* Parklane Hosiery Co. v. Shore, 439 U.S. 322 (1979). Although non-judicial determinations such as agency decisions are less formal than judicial proceedings, courts have given a preclusive effect to such decisions when it is shown that there was an opportunity to fully and fairly litigate the issue. *E.g.* Bowen v. United

States, 570 F.2d 1311, 1322 (7th Cir. 1978); Campbell v. Superior Court, 18 Ariz.App. 287, 501 P.2d 463 (1972). *See also, e.g.,* University of Tennessee v. Elliott, 478 U.S. 788 (1986) (in Title VII claim, federal courts must give preclusive effect to fact finding of state administrative body acting in judicial capacity).

It has been held, for example, that a decision by an NASD arbitration panel should be given preclusive effect in federal court. Hammerman v. Peacock, 654 F.Supp. 71 (D.D.C. 1987). This result is especially justifiable in light of the Supreme Court's reasoning in *McMahon*. The same result should follow under the FINRA arbitration rules.

One problem with arbitration awards is that they rarely indicate the precise basis for the decision. *See, e.g.,* Trustees of Lawrence Academy v. Merrill Lynch, Pierce, Fenner & Smith, Inc., 821 F.Supp. 59 (D.N.H. 1993) (arbitrators are not required to make findings of fact nor give reasons for their award). Accordingly, it may frequently be difficult to establish the scope of preclusive effect to be given. In such a case, unless res judicata (claim preclusion) applies, it may not be possible to invoke collateral estoppel (issue preclusion). In order for issue preclusion to be invoked, the issue in both the first and second litigation must be the same. Therefore, where the arbitrator's award does not reveal the basis of the decision, collateral estoppel is not appropriate.

§ 90. Review of Court Orders Compelling or Denying Arbitration or Staying Judicial Proceedings

Prior to 1989, difficult questions arose with regard to the ability to appeal a court order compelling arbitration or staying further judicial proceedings pending arbitration. However, FAA § 15 now provides that such orders are not subject to interlocutory review unless the trial judge certifies the order for review. In contrast, interlocutory orders denying arbitration or refusing a stay of a judicial action pending arbitration are subject to interlocutory review without certification by the trial judge. This lack of parallelism reflects the strong federal policy favoring arbitration by readily permitting interlocutory review to preserve the right to arbitrate.

§ 91. Judicial Review of Arbitration Decisions

Arbitration decisions under the federal securities laws are reviewable by federal district courts. In addition to the statutory grounds of corruption, fraud, and evident partiality, arbitration decisions are subject to the judicially created standard of "manifest disregard of the law." Some decisions have spoken in terms of a "clearly erroneous" or "completely irrational" standard for judicial review of arbitration decisions. Thus, the scope of judicial review is extremely limited. In furtherance of the strong federal policy supporting arbitration, the courts give considerable deference to the arbitrator's decision. In order to overturn a decision, courts generally require an "obvious" error, which "clearly means more than error or misunderstanding with respect to the law." Merrill Lynch, Pierce, Fenner & Smith v. Bobker, 808 F.2d 930, 933 (2d Cir. 1986). It has thus been held, for example, that an arbitration award should not be vacated unless it can be shown that the arbitrator "deliberately ignored" the applicable statutory and SEC regulatory provisions. Id.

APPENDIX

FURTHER READING

Thomas Lee Hazen, Treatise on the Law of Securities Regulation (West 6th ed. 2009)

Thomas Lee Hazen, Hornbook on the Law of Securities Regulation (West 6th ed. 2009)

Thomas Lee Hazen & David L. Ratner, Broker–Dealer Regulation Cases and Materials (West 2003)

Jerry W. Markham & Thomas L. Hazen, Broker–Dealer Operations Under Securities and Commodities Law: Financial Responsibilities, Credit Regulation, and Customer Protection (West 2d ed. 2003)

Thomas Lee Hazen, Securities Regulation in a Nutshell (West 10th ed. 2009)

GLOSSARY

AFTER MARKET—Once shares in a public offering get into the hands of investors, the trades taking place between investors or traders are after-market transactions.

BLUE SKY LAW—Blue sky law is a term used to refer to state securities laws.

BOILER ROOM—Boiler room refers to a brokerage firm that focuses on high pressure sales practices and various fraudulent activities.

BUCKET SHOP—A variety of boiler room where the customer orders are not actually placed. The orders are bucketed rather than entered in the markets.

CALL OPTION—A call option is a contract between a seller (the option writer) and a buyer under which the option buyer has the right to exercise the option and thereby purchase the underlying security at an agreed-on price (the "strike" or "exercise" price). The option will expire unexercised (and hence valueless) unless it is exercised within a specified time period, the last day of which is the expiration date. *See also* "put option."

CHURNING—Churning is an illegal practice when brokers with discretionary authority or control over an account enter into trades to generate commissions.

COLLAR—A collar is an option strategy designed to limit the downside risk or upside potential of a security.

CROSS TRADE—*See* "matched order."

FLIPPING—Flipping occurs when someone purchases securities as part of a public offering with an intent to sell immediately into a rising after-market.

FREE WRITING—Free writing refers to information not contained in a prospectus relating to a company that may be disseminated by a company engaged in a public offering.

GUN JUMPING—Gun jumping results from premature publicity about an upcoming public offering. Gun jumping is prohibited by 1933 Act § 5(c).

HAIRCUT—Haircut is a discount deducted from the value of securities when computing value for purposes of the net capital requirements for securities broker-dealers (SEC Rule 15c3–1).

MARGIN—A margin transaction involves buying securities with funds borrowed from the broker. The Federal Reserve Board and the exchanges set the minimum margin requirements.

MARKET MAKER—A market maker is a securities dealer that provides firm bid and asked prices for securities. Market makers are regulated by FIN-RA and originally functioned primarily in the over-the-counter markets but now also make a market for exchange traded securities.

MARKING THE CLOSE—Marking the close is a manipulative practice whereby a portfolio manager artificially inflates the price of stocks held in the portfolio just before the close of trading for the purpose of increasing the portfolio's value.

MARK–UP (and MARK–DOWN)—A mark-up or mark-down refers to the commission received by a broker-dealer for a retail transaction in the NASDAQ market. A mark-up represents the amount that the customer is charged above the actual purchase price. A mark-down is the amount deducted from the proceeds of the sales price.

MATCHED ORDER—A "matched" order occurs when orders are entered simultaneously to buy and sell the same security. The mere fact that a broker crosses trades or enters into matched orders does not violate the 1934 Act. In fact, cross-trades can actually benefit the firm's customers if the savings on commissions are passed on to the customers. However, the cross-trades become problematic when the cost savings are not passed on to the customer.

ODD–LOT—An odd-lot refers to a block of shares under 100. Traditionally shares in publicly held companies have been traded 100 share lots. Transactions in hundred share lots are referred to as round lots.

OVER–THE–COUNTER—An over-the-counter transaction is one that takes place other than through the facilities of an organized securities exchange.

PAINTING THE TAPE—Painting the tape is a manipulative practice of reporting fictitious orders to make it appear that real transactions are taking place.

PARKING—Parking is a fraudulent practice of parking shares in someone else's name in order to hide the identity of the true owner.

POST–EFFECTIVE PERIOD—The post-effective period is the time after a 1933 Act registration has become effective. Sales of the securities covered by the registration statement are not permitted until the beginning of the post-effective period. During the post-effective period, the prospectus delivery requirements of 1933 Act §§ 5(b), 10 continue to apply.

PREFILING PERIOD—The prefiling period is that time shortly before the filing of a registration when all offers to buy and all offers to sell are prohibited by the terms of 1933 Act § 5(a).

PROXY—A power of attorney from a shareholder authorizing the proxy holder to vote the shares owned by a shareholder. *Proxy* is defined in SEC Rule 14a–1(f) to include any shareholder's consent or authorization regarding the casting of that shareholder's vote. Requirements for the appropriate form of the proxy itself can be found in Rule 14a–4.

PROXY STATEMENT—A proxy statement is the mandated venue for management's solicitation of proxies. See SEC Schedule 14A.

PROSPECTUS—As defined in 1933 Act § 2(a)(10) is a written offer to sell or one made through other permanent means such as online. During a public offering, a prospectus is subject to the disclosure requirements spelled out in § 10. Also § 5(b) sets forth the circumstances under which a prospectus must be provided to investors.

PROXY SOLICITATION—Solicitation, as defined in SEC Rule 14a–1(*l*), includes the following: any request for a proxy; any request to execute or not to execute, or to revoke, a proxy; or any communication to shareholders reasonably calculated to result in the procurement, withholding, or revocation of a proxy. Rule 14a–1(*l*). Rule 14a–2 lists the types of solicitations exempt from the proxy rules. Rule 14a–2. Rule 14a–3 sets forth the types of information that must be included in proxy solicitations. Rule 14a–3.

PUMP AND DUMP—A pump and dump scheme is the fraudulent and manipulative practice of hyping particular stocks to bring them to artificially high levels and then dumping the stock into the market.

PUT OPTION—A put option gives the option's buyer the right to exercise the option by selling the underlying security. The put-option seller must purchase the underlying security at the agreed-on price if the option is exercised on or before the expiration date. If the strike price is "out of the money" in comparison with the price of the underlying security, so that it would not make economic sense to exercise the option, the option will simply expire unexercised. *See also* "call option."

QUIET PERIOD—The quiet period is the time shortly before a 1933 Act registration statement is filed in connection with a public offering (also known as the prefiling period). During the quiet period participants in the offering must be careful not to disseminate information that could be construed as an illegal offer to sell the securities to be covered by the registration statement.

RED HERRING PROSPECTUS—A red herring prospectus is a preliminary prospectus that may be used after the filing of a 1933 Act registration during the waiting period. *See* SEC Rule 430.

REPORTING COMPANY—A reporting company is a publicly held company that is subject to the 1934 Act's periodic (annual, quarterly, and interim) reporting requirements. Reporting companies include those having to register under 1934 Act § 12 because their shares are listed on a national exchange (including the NYSE, AMEX, and NAS-DAQ Stock Market) as well as over-the-counter companies having more than $10 million in assets and 500 shareholders of record.

RESTRICTED SECURITIES—A restricted security is one that is subject to transfer restrictions. Restricted securities often result from securities that are sold in a private placement as opposed to a public offering.

SAFE HARBOR RULE—A safe harbor rule is a rule under which the SEC provides guidance as to how to comply with specific provisions of the securities laws. It is a safe harbor but is not the exclusive way of complying with the applicable law.

SALE AGAINST THE BOX—A "sale against the box" takes place when the seller, anticipating a decline in the price of stock she owns, sells it to a buyer at the present market price, but delivers it later, when (she hopes) the market price will have fallen below the sales price, thus creating a paper profit for the seller.

SCALPING—Scalping is the illegal practice that occurs when someone touts securities that he owns with the goal of raising the price to increase the value of his holdings.

SECONDARY OFFERING—A secondary offering occurs when securities are offered as part of a distribution by existing securities holders. In a secondary offering the proceeds of the sale go to the selling shareholders. In contrast, with a primary offering the shares are sold by the issuer and the proceeds go to the company.

SHELF REGISTRATION—A shelf registration is a 1933 Act registration statement for securities that are going to be offered on a delayed or continuous basis. *See* SEC Rule 415.

SHORT SALE—A "short sale" takes place when a seller, believing the price of a stock will fall, borrows stock from a lender and sells it to a buyer. Later, the seller buys similar stock to pay back the lender, ideally at a lower price than he received on the sale to the buyer.

SOLICITATION—*See Proxy* solicitation.

SPECIALIST—For most of its existence, New York Stock Exchange trading took place through specialist firms who had no retail securities business. Over time the specialist system is giving way to a system based on designated market makers who function much like market makers in the over-the-counter markets.

SPREAD—The spread is the difference between the bid and the asked price of a security. A market maker makes its commission through the spread—by buying at the bid price and then selling the securities at the asked price. *See also* mark-up and mark-down.

SPREAD (OPTIONS STRATEGY)—A spread is an option strategy of purchasing and selling an equal number of options with different strike prices or different expiration dates. This strategy is also sometimes referred to as a straddle.

STRADDLE—See spread (options strategy).

STREET NAME—Securities are held in street name when the brokerage firm holds the securities in their own name for the benefit of the customer as beneficial owner.

TOMBSTONE ADVERTISEMENT—A tombstone ad is the industry term for an identifying statement that simply announces the offering and lists the underwriter.

UNDERWRITER—An underwriter is a broker-dealer or investment banking firm that acts as a wholesaler for a securities distribution. Underwriter status can also result from substantial participation in a securities distribution. *See* 1933 Act § 2(a)(11).

WAITING PERIOD—The waiting period is the time between the filing a 1933 Act registration statement is filed and the time that it becomes effective. Sales of the securities covered by the registration statement are no permitted during the waiting period (1933 Act § 5(a)). Also, during the waiting period, written, online, radio, and television communications must satisfy or be exempt from the prospectus requirements of 1933 Act §§ 5(b), 10.

WARRANT—A warrant is a stock option issued by the company itself often as compensation to promoters or as a separate security to be publicly traded. Stock options may also be issued by the company to employees or consultants; these are generally simply referred to as stock options and not as warrants.

WASH SALE—A "wash" sale is a fictitious sale where there is no change in beneficial ownership: It is a transaction without the usual profit motive and is designed to give the false impression of market activity when in fact there is none.

INDEX

References are to Sections

---

†